A Portrait of an African Grey

What To Expect When You Live With Large Birds

by

Dru & Al Simon

A Portrait of Dorian Grey

What To Expect When You Live With Large Birds

by

Dru and Al Simon

MMXII

Copyright 2012 by Dru and Al Simon

All Rights Reserved

ISBN-13:
9781480222724
ISBN-10:
1480222720

Printed in the United States of America

This book has no connection to Oscar Wilde's famous novel, "The Picture of Dorian Gray" (1890), though it will immediately be clear to the reader that we named our African Grey Parrot Dorian in amused homage to that story. The bird himself has never made any protest over the pun, though admittedly, he's never read the story.

TABLE OF CONTENTS

DISCLAIMER VIII
INTRODUCTION IX
YOUR BASIC AFRICAN GREY PARROT XI
SOME CAUTIONARY NOTES XII
YOU WON'T ENJOY LIVING WITH A PARROT, COCKATOO, MACAW, OR OTHER PSITTICINE IF: XVI
BUT IT'S NOT ALL BAD NEWS! XVII
PART ONE 1
A BRIEF BIOGRAPHY OF A SMALL, FEATHERED AUTOCRAT 1
SO, HOW DID WE END UP WITH PARROTS, OF ALL PETS? 2
WHAT'S A "BAPPY"? 4
A "BIRD CAVE" OF HIS OWN 11
GROWING UP IS HARD TO DO (ESPECIALLY ON US!) 15
DORIAN'S RELATIONSHIP WITH EACH OF US 19
THE DAILY ROUTINE 22
CROSSING THE COUNTRY WITH THREE UNEASY BIRDS 26
GETTING USED TO THE NEW PLACE 31
WHY "DORIE THE DUCK"? 35
PART TWO – CARE, FEEDING, AND REQUIRED DAILY ABJECT WORSHIPPING 36

BASIC CHARACTERISTICS OF THE AFRICAN GREY PARROT 37

NOW, THIS WON'T HURT A BIT… 41

PROVIDING A PROPER BIRD HOME 48

CLEANING THE CAGE, THE PLAYPEN, THE FLOOR, AND YOURSELF 54

EATING IS A SOCIAL EVENT! 62

HOW TO POISON A PARROT 68

WHY DORIAN HAS NEVER LEARNED TO SAY "EXCUSE ME" 71

BIRD ETIQUETTE – RULES THE FLOCK MUST FOLLOW (THIS INCLUDES YOU) 72

INSTINCTIVE FEARS 82

DOES HE TALK? THE QUESTION IS, DOES HE EVER SHUT UP?! 86

THE TRANSFORMATION OF WORDS 94

YES, THEY'RE THINKING AND REASONING. MY FAVORITE EXAMPLES 96

BIRDS' MOST IMPORTANT LANGUAGE – BODY LANGUAGE 102

TERRITORIAL & MANIPULATIVE BEHAVIOR 109

TRAUMATIC BEHAVIOR 111

v

ENDEARING BEHAVIOR 115

THEY'RE TIDY ON THEIR OWN TERMS 119

PREENING – WHAT IT'S REALLY ABOUT 124

MORNING IS FLOCK TIME 131

AFTERNOON IS NAP TIME 133

IS HE SCHIZOPHRENIC DURING BREEDING TIME? WELL, YES AND NO! 135

TOYS AND OTHER AMUSEMENTS 138

THE MOUTH AND THE FOOT ARE THE HANDS 147

SO DON'T KID YOURSELF; YOU WILL BE BITTEN! 151

WHY WE STICK-TRAINED THE BIRDS 153

WHEN THE CAT'S AWAY THE BIRD WILL PLAY 155

OBEDIENCE – OR – YOU THINK HERDING CATS IS HARD? 157

THE MOST DIFFICULT CONCEPTS TO TEACH A BIRD 159

THE MOST DIFFICULT CONCEPTS TO TEACH A BIRD OWNER 162

"SOMEBODY STOP ME – I WANT TO KILL THAT BIRD!!" 164

THE PUNISHMENT NEVER REALLY FITS THE CRIME 167

KNOWING WHEN TO CALL IT QUITS 172

A BRIEF WORD ABOUT ROVER AND POLGARA 176

AN EVEN BRIEFER WORD ABOUT BIRDS WITH OTHER PETS 179

THE RULES OF LIFE AS SET OUT BY BIRDS 181

DORIAN'S COMMON-USE VOCABULARY 183

DORIAN'S MOST COMMON PHRASES 185

JUST A FEW OF THE MANY, MANY EXCELLENT ONLINE AND HARD COPY RESOURCES FOR INFORMATION ABOUT COMPANION PARROTS 187

DISCLAIMER

First and foremost we need to make clear that my husband Al and I are NOT vets, ornithologists, or avian behaviorists. Our knowledge about our birds comes from living with them along with independent research and consultations with real vets, real avian behaviorists, and other credentialed experts. The views expressed in this book are our personal opinions, based on our own research and experience with our birds and should not be taken as gospel over the advice or information given by vets or other avian experts.

INTRODUCTION

Our aim in writing this book is two-fold. First and foremost we want to educate anyone interested in living with companion parrots as to the realities of doing so, which are nothing whatsoever like the realities of living with other pet species. There are over 400 bird sanctuaries and rescue facilities in the U.S. and they are always filled nearly to capacity because people adopt these amazing but demanding animals without knowing enough about them beforehand. They are NOT in any way, shape, or form like dogs or cats, and this book attempts to describe in a humorous and enjoyable way both the joys and the burdens of living with parrots and other, similar birds.

Our second reason for writing the book (with some difficulty because Dorian keeps walking over the keyboard) is that parrots are very long-lived, and Congo African Grey parrots are no exception. As I write this, our mischievous, marvelous, demanding, delightful and often quite astounding parrot is only 19 years old, and can expect to live well past my own present age of 62. Because birds take to change more unhappily than we humans do, we're setting down this history of our life with Dorian as background, and hope the rest of the book will ultimately serve as a kind of "Owner's Manual" for the benefit of whomever will be the center of his world once we're gone.

We hope the advice and guidance we provide in this work will be of great use to anyone who lives with or is considering living with a companion parrot, macaw, conure, or any of the other species in the psitticine family.

YOUR BASIC AFRICAN GREY PARROT

Like the typical Congo African Grey, Dorian is about 12 inches from the tip of his red tail to the top of his grey head. This is somewhat of an estimate since whenever I try to measure him he invariably twists his head upward to nibble on the ruler or measuring tape.

You can read a lot from many sources all about Greys. There are many books, and the Internet abounds with sites from the dry factual to the fascinating accounts of Irene Pepperberg's extraordinary African Grey Alex but you'll never really get to know what these birds are like unless you live with one. This is something we recommend AGAINST unless you're seriously committed to putting up with the never-ending mess, noise, and demands as well as the fascination and affection of these unrelenting tyrants who will love you forever but on THEIR terms according to the rules set by the birds themselves millions of years ago.

It's interesting to note that the life expectancy for African Greys is cited differently in different sources. One source claims they live between 40 and 60 years, while another (within the same article) claims their span is between 60 and 90 years. We've even heard that they can live for over 100 years. In my personal opinion this disparity probably comes from people who live with these birds; therefore it only SEEMS as though they live forever…

SOME CAUTIONARY NOTES

In case this book inspires you to run out and purchase or adopt an African Grey Parrot (or any other companion bird), we must reiterate not only for your sake but for the sake of the bird - that living with parrots is in NO WAY anything like living with dogs or cats.

Just consider the most basic fact: dogs, cats, and humans are predators. We have binocular vision for hunting and specialized teeth for tearing into and chewing up our food.

Birds are prey animals. Their eyes are on the sides of their head, providing them with 360 degrees of vision so they can see us predators coming from any direction. They don't have teeth at all but rub their food against the upper portion of their beak (called the maxillary rostrum, in case you think there's going to be a quiz later…there won't be). Because of this very basic difference birds (and other prey animals) see the world from a very different point of view. Just for one example, we predators don't think much about things like potentially being eaten by another creature. Prey animals think about it all the time.

Another difference between dog or cats and birds is how long-lived birds are. You need to understand that having a companion parrot is a LIFE-LONG COMMITMENT! They need constant care – you can't just play with them when it suits you and ignore them the rest of the time. They're flock creatures – they NEED to be with the flock (that means YOU). Also, while they live as long as we do they never grow past the emotional development of a human two year old. Yes, it's like living with someone in their "Terrible Twos" for SIXTY or more years! They are very demanding of attention; they want to eat what and when you eat, they want to trumpet and peep and shout when they feel like it despite the movie you're watching, the studying you have to do, the visiting in-laws you're trying to impress, or the IRS agent you have on the phone.

Also, the mess factor is a major issue. Dogs eat pretty much in two areas: their own dish and at your side at the dinner table in begging position. Cats eat primarily from their food bowl with discretionary forays into rodent, bird, or bug-catching, with the added bonus of having them sometimes present their kill to you as a loving gift. Charming. (Don't get me wrong – we adore dogs and cats and lived with both for many years.)

Now think about wild birds, living in the forests, jungles and deserts all over the world. Part of their role in nature is to spread seeds throughout their environment so new trees and plants will grow. How do they accomplish this? THEY THROW FOOD. A simple but true fact. Birds will take a big piece of food (and wild parrots eat mostly fruits, nuts and seeds along with some greenery), nibble at some of it, then either toss their head to throw away what they don't want or simply drop the leftovers in favor of a new and more exciting tidbit.

Now picture this behavior occurring on your nice, deep pile, light beige carpet. Because it will. There is no known way of preventing birds from tossing food except perhaps cutting what you feed them into tiny, pea-sized morsels so they don't have enough left to throw. Even then they'll pick it out of their bowl and toss it away if they see a more interesting bit of food beneath it. I'm talking DAILY vacuuming or sweeping or both. Sometimes performed multiple times a day. A cartoon created **by Janet Bray** of **Birdbrain Gifts** said it all: "Living With Parrots: It's kinda like having a blender with no lid that's always on." Disbelieve this at your peril!

Lastly, there's the noise factor — never to be overlooked! One of the "bird rules" is that one's presence is to be announced in the morning and in the evening so other birds within THE ENTIRE NEIGHBORHOOD will know where flock members are and which trees they'd better avoid because it's been claimed by another bird. When you wake up in the morning and hear the twittering and calling from tree to tree in your neighborhood, what you're hearing is a sort of roll-call. One bird will announce his presence and listen for the calls of flock members or birds of other species or flocks so everyone knows where everyone else is. It's quite pleasant when you're listening to robins and starlings and larks, with the occasional crow thrown in for good measure. Now think about where parrots live. In dense rainforests or jungles and widely spread trees in the Australian desert. In order for them to be heard in the morning reveille their voices have to be exceedingly LOUD. The fact that they now live in a corner of your living room has no bearing on the volume at which they will announce themselves to the world every morning; nor do they have any respect for alarm clocks, work schedules, or how late you got to bed the previous evening.

But that's just the morning call. At around sunset they once more call out, again to identify themselves to the surrounding avian neighbors, telling everyone it's time for bed and please not to come near their nesting spot but choose another and leave them to go to sleep.

It matters not at all if your schedule differs from theirs — birds need about 12 hours of sleep every night and if someone wonderful is on the late-night talk show on the TV they may make a verbal complaint to management (you) once in a while that you're disturbing them. There is no way to curtail this behavior. It's normal. Each bird species has its own set of calls and while some may not be too loud or too long, they are inevitable and unstoppable. You have to live with it.

Following is a checklist to help you determine if a companion psitticine is the wrong pet for you:

YOU WON'T ENJOY LIVING WITH A PARROT, COCKATOO, MACAW, OR OTHER PSITTICINE IF:

~Loud noises bother you

~Messy eaters upset you

~You object to or are unable to sweep, clean or vacuum daily (walls sometimes included)

~You don't like sharing your food

~You think cutting up a variety of fresh fruits, nuts, and vegetables for the bird every morning is insane

~You live in an apartment with thin walls (you'll hear from your neighbors quite often)

~You object to being bitten on occasion

~You do NOT have patience or a forgiving nature

~You lack a broad sense of humor

~You travel a lot; thus spending a lot of time away from the home "flock"

~You're not able to devote a large percentage of your time to interacting with the bird

~You don't think you can live for the next 40 years with a creature who never, ever grows out of the "Terrible Twos"

~You're not willing to constantly pick up after, train, or discipline a bird.

~You're looking for a pet that wants nothing more than to please you

BUT IT'S NOT ALL BAD NEWS!

Don't get me wrong - despite the list of caveats, birds can and do behave in adorable, startling, impressive, affectionate and irresistible ways, making you suddenly forgive the way they woke you up when they loudly warned you that the postman just drove by. All Dorian has to do is look at me and say, "Dorie Good Bird – Big Kiss!" and little hearts appear in my eyes and I melt all over again.

In many ways birds are much like young humans. An interesting thing I've noticed is that Rover (our Umbrella Cocaktoo) and Polgara (our Orange-Winged Amazon Parrot) become disturbed by scary or threatening background music when we're watching a movie or a show on TV. They'll make protesting or worried calls until the music stops or changes, or until we lower it until it no longer sounds threatening.

Polgara and Rover on a play gym

Oh yes – birds are very responsive to music! Our flock enjoys a wide spectrum of musical genres, and in fact Polgara actually sings along with opera – she has a decided preference for baritones.

Dorian reacts differently. If he hears us commenting on a program, having English as his first language, he tends to comment along with us or laugh if he hears us laughing. Not all his comments are intelligible – much like a 2 year old human who babbles to himself in imitation of what he hears adults saying. His laughter however is genuine enough to make others laugh along with him, and while he can't carry a tune very well, he loves to sing and listen to music with us.

Most birds are responsive to music, and each individual expresses its appreciation in its own unique way. Some easily pick up lyrics (though not always the melody) of favorite songs and need little or no encouragement to break out in song. Others will dance to favorite songs, beats, or bands. A perfect example is the famous and utterly delightful **Snowball**, a Medium Sulphur-Crested Eleanora Cockatoo who lives with **Irena and Charles Schulz**, the founders of the **Bird Lovers Only** rescue facility in South Carolina. Look up their website at www.birdloversonly.org and view some of the videos of Snowball dancing away. You'll be amazed and enchanted. I promise!

As you read our account of our life with Dorian, Polgara, and Rover please keep in mind that every bird is an individual, as is every human. The things Dorian regularly does may be something another African Grey will never do. This diversity is one of the reasons living with psitticines is so fascinating, amusing, wonderful, and demanding. There's so much to learn about the intriguing and often startling world of birds and being part of a flock. We hope you'll find the following interesting, informative, amusing, and of value to you and your own flock of amazing and wonderful companions.

PART ONE

A BRIEF BIOGRAPHY OF A SMALL, FEATHERED AUTOCRAT**

** We refer to Dorian as an Autocrat because in his mind he is the absolute ruler of the roost. He cannot conceive of not getting whatever he wants as soon as he wants it. Trying to make him understand the error of this thinking is a CONSTANT process.

SO, HOW DID WE END UP WITH PARROTS, OF ALL PETS?

It's really simple. Over the years Al and I have owned several wonderful dogs and cats – all of whom were short-lived in comparison to ourselves. As anyone who's shared their life with a companion animal knows, their inevitable loss is as painful as the loss of any human companion – sometimes more so. After the heartbreaking death of our 17 year old Siamese cat, Piwacket (named after the cat in the movie, *"Bell, Book, and Candle"*) we wanted more pets but couldn't face the loss of another four-legged family member.

1Reh, our calico angora

Fosdick, Old English Sheepdog

Piwacket, Frost Point Siamese

Avatar, Orange Persian

Large birds were the answer.

Oh, wait – I can happily blame this on our daughter Rachael, who after Piwacket's death decided she wanted a pair of parakeets for her 12th birthday. Now, the average lifespan of a parakeet is about 10 years, so we left the budgies to her and thought about longer-lived birds. That opened the way for us to rescue Rover the Umbrella Cockatoo and Polgara the Orange Winged Amazon Parrot, (see their photos a few pages back) both of whom had been abused and were quite a handful for the first several years that we owned them. Their care has been an education in itself but let me focus on the main character of this book – our darling, our tyrant, the bane and blessing of our existence; Mr. Dorian Gray, our Congo African Grey Parrot.

Who, me??

WHAT'S A "BAPPY"?

In 1992 **Sally Blanchard**, bird expert, creator of articles, reports and websites dedicated to companion birds, and author of ***The Companion Parrot Handbook*** coined the word "bappy" in an article in issue #6 of the ***Pet Bird Report***, using it as a descriptive word for baby parrots; just as baby cats are kittens and baby dogs are puppies. Yes, the most common word for a baby bird is "chick" but that applies just as well to a baby vulture or turkey or hummingbird. Since parrots are special in our hearts, why not provide a special name for them when they're babies? Ms. Blanchard has received both congratulations and condemnation for the coining of this word but since it rhymes with the word "happy" (Ms. Blanchard's intent) we've always used "bappy" as an endearment for all our birds.

So there we were, the owners of two parakeets, a neurotic male Umbrella Cockatoo and a highly aggressive Amazon Parrot; struggling to tame and comfort these creatures while learning their ways and studying up on the proper care and feeding of all four of them.

It was in the summer of 1993; only a year or three after we rescued Rover and Pol that a colleague of mine obtained a five week old African Grey Parrot and desperately wanted to find it a home. Naturally he viewed us as ~~suckers~~ – uh, kind-hearted and experienced bird people, so he approached us. Unable to resist the "awwww" factor of a small, baby bird who looked at us with dark, innocent and hopeful eyes, we handed over a fistful of fairly large-denomination dollar bills, took the new baby home with us, and named him Dorian. Well, it was either Dorian Grey or Zane Grey, and since I was never a fan of "old west" novels, Dorian it had to be.

There we stood, gazing at the innocent little thing – just fledged but not fully grown – so young he didn't know how to stand on a perch but huddled on the bottom of the small cage in which we'd brought him home. We had already obtained an avian vet for our other family members (not all vets are <u>expert</u> at caring for birds) so a quick visit assured us of his health and supplied us with careful instructions on the care and feeding of a bird too young to know how to crack seed shells.

From the beginning we gave Dorian a lot of petting and stroking to get him used to physical contact with us (cuddling by a recognized predator is not something that comes all that easily to many birds) and this made him special to us right away, since Rover was too traumatized by his previous abuse to trust our hands at that time and Polgara's reaction to the abuse she had endured was to become even more aggressive and bold than Amazons are under normal circumstances. This difference in treatment also put a wedge in the relationship between Dorian and the other birds that remains to this day, since he clearly was treated differently than they were. It's our thing about not wanting to have our hands bitten...

Now, you may ask, "if Dorian was too young to know how to crack seeds, what did he eat"? Well, as you've no doubt seen in countless wildlife documentaries, baby birds are fed food their parents have generously pre-digested for them and regurgitate into their eager little mouths.

Mother bird feeding her baby

Of course humans can't do that for their pets (and in fact, just the thought makes me want to regurgitate in a *bad, non-nutritious* way) but there are several excellent baby-bird foods available in most pet stores. This is a powder one mixes with warm water until it's the consistency of loose oatmeal or thick gravy. We were instructed by our avian vet to make it more palatable by adding an equal amount of strained fruit from any reputable baby food company. One then loads up a feeding syringe with this mush and slowly injects it into baby's eager mouth. This worked fine with the small exception that Dorie was not at all a neat eater. Between his eagerness to feed and his inexperience at dealing with the syringe he often wore more food than he swallowed.

Oh, believe me, cleaning that stuff off bird feathers is neither easy nor fun, especially since the baby didn't like the warm, wet washcloth with which I afterward tried to clean him. He struggled and wiggled and bit throughout the entire process.

Eventually we solved the problem by wrapping him in clear plastic wrap with only his head free, and he never minded the confinement. At least that's what I prefer to think. In either case, not knowing how silly this made him look, he readily allowed us to wrap him like a tuna sandwich several times a day. This looked ridiculous but it made the frequent feedings much, much easier.

A lot of experts offer detailed instructions on how to insert the syringe just right and how to watch for the baby's crop (food storage area) to fill up and so forth but we just slowly injected the food into his mouth and let him figure out how and when to swallow it. It seemed to work all right for us and he never choked or got overfull.

Frequent feedings are part of every infant's care, no matter the species and we kept a careful schedule until he was old enough to start learning to eat solid foods. I think we went through half a giant roll of plastic wrap before he was completely weaned.

During this time Al played the role of "Mommy Bird". He was the primary feeder, washer, tickler, praiser, cuddler, and provider of health and safety. He had high hopes of being the center of Dorian's universe, and while the bird was young, he was indeed. Dorie loved Al to distraction! During his "bappy-hood" he absolutely doted on his "Mommy Bird".

For example, any time Al wanted to nap, the bird would perch on his shoulder and guard him from the world. It was almost guaranteed that anyone coming near would be threatened by suddenly spread wings, a beak lunge and a squawky sort of growl.

Young Dorian guarding (young) Al during a nap

Eventually we knew we had to wean him off baby-bird food but I don't recall exactly how old he was - it varies from bird to bird and some African Greys are fed by their parents for six to nine months! We started to put various seeds and fruits in a bowl in his cage, and being a curious little fellow he explored it all but it was about six months before he started to prefer solid food over the baby food. (though he's 19 now I sometimes suspect that if we offered him the syringe again he might enjoy not having to do the 'work' of feeding himself. A great hunter/forager he is NOT).

His propensity for speech was a decided benefit in his eating habits because he quickly learned the names of his preferred foods. Nowadays he unabashedly asks for them…all day long.

As time went by Dorian learned how to crack open seeds and developed his taste for apples, kiwi, and other nutritious food items…like M&Ms (yes, we know chocolate isn't good for him. It isn't good for us humans, either but we all love it anyway, don't we?). Like all children he'd much prefer cake and ice cream to his usual healthy diet. This is why I feed all three of our birds with a nutritious "pelleted" food along with cut up fruits, chopped vegetables, pastas and grains and a few nuts in the mornings and leave other foods and treats for later in the day.

Let's face it: if you set a breakfast in front of your child consisting of scrambled eggs, toast, juice, a candy bar, some popcorn, and an ice cream sundae, which do you think the child is going to eat? Of course. So would I. (admit it; you would too).

Birds (and I suppose all animals) are the same. If they (or we) lived out in the wild it would make a lot of sense to fill up on high calorie food like nuts and seeds because it would be used up searching for more food and avoiding predators. Since we and our pets live in a culture where all sorts of food is readily available we have to ignore our predilection for chocolate, sunflower seeds and Boston Cream Pie and feed ourselves and our pets sensibly. Or at least, try to do so…

Anyway, as time went by Dorian thrived and learned to speak, how to interact with his flock (us and the other two birds) and how to fly. Well, SORT OF how to fly. See, he had no avian parents to demonstrate this important skill for him. Yes, there are two other birds in our flock however they don't spend much time in flight either. You see, Psittaciformes (parrots, cockatoos, macaws, parakeets, lorikeets, conures, lovebirds etc.) are natural energy savers. They'd rather sit than walk, they'd rather walk than run, and they'd rather run than fly, so they reserve flight for emergencies, which don't often occur within the confines of a six foot by six foot by three foot cage unless one loses one's footing and falls off the perch. Yeah, it happens.

Well, Dorie figured those wings were for SOME purpose, so he flapped and exercised them and jumped with the best of them until he learned how to take off and gain a little altitude. At first he was fairly good at flying short distances however it took him a little longer to figure out how to land. For the first year of his life Dorian broke off tail feathers so often that all he had were his short, red, contour feathers that lie over the long tail feathers. Yeah, he looked pretty silly for a while there.

At last he figured it all out and now he can land on a dime but knowing him, he'd probably try to eat it.

A "BIRD CAVE" OF HIS OWN

African Greys, along with most psitticines need a special place of their own where they can hide and rest. Dorian obtained his in a fairly terrible way, poor fellow.

When he first came into our lives we lived in the northwest corner of the San Fernando Valley which is just north of Los Angeles. He was hatched on July 14th (Bastille Day, which I think is ironic) 1993 and therefore was only six months old when the infamous Northridge Earthquake struck on January 17th, 1994. The town we lived in was the next town over from Northridge so we were only about five miles from the epicenter of that horrible event. If you've never been in a large earthquake I should tell you that while small quakes feel like a large truck just rattled by your front door, a large one, such as the one Northridge suffered, is a whole different story.

Let me explain what it's like in this way: If you've ever bought a gallon of paint in a home improvement store, think about the machine they put the can onto that mixes the color you've chosen.

Just a small sample of the damage our house sustained during the 1994 Northridge Earthquake

It violently shakes that can back and forth and up and down until the color is just right. Now imagine yourself INSIDE that paint can! I can honestly say that the 33 seconds of the Northridge quake were the worst of my life. The sound itself was horrific – the world rumbled and boomed so loudly you could hardly hear your own shouting. It was fortunate that the quake occurred in the middle of the night, because most people were in bed and like us, holding on for dear life so they wouldn't get thrown onto the floor. Things flew off shelves – roofs and chimneys and walls fell down, furniture was thrown over, pictures were knocked off walls – and poor, six month old Dorian was alone…

I still feel badly about it. You see, since Al was "Mommy Bird" he had Dorian with him in his office most of the time so Dorian lived and slept in a typical parrot cage situated in Al's office on the ground floor of our two-story home.

During the quake not only was he shaken around in his cage but a large, glass-covered picture that had hung next to his cage was thrown off the wall and struck the cage as it broke. Happily, none of the glass ended up inside the cage but imagine the poor baby bird's terror as he was not only shaken about and surrounded by horrific noise, but the picture from the wall literally attacked him!

Of course, after the quake we dressed and hurried down to survey the damage (and boy, was there damage!) and see how the birds had fared. Rover and Polgara were all right – their cage wasn't near anything that had fallen over but little Dorian was seriously terrified and traumatized, though happily, he wasn't physically injured (none of us were).

During the next two weeks as we cleaned up the mess and endured multiple, large aftershocks (the large ones continued for about half a year after the quake) Dorian clung to Al in every way; peeping unhappily if his Mommy Bird even disappeared to go to the bathroom for five minutes. The poor baby was unable to sleep unless he was in physical contact with Al, which, as you can imagine, could NOT continue indefinitely because Al was losing sleep worrying that he might roll over onto Dorian and crush him.

At last we consulted our veterinarian who suggested we do what she did with her own bird, which was to purchase a Kennel Cab; one of those portable, plastic cages in which one sometimes sees dogs or cats being carried. Per her instructions we installed a perch, a small ladder and a few toys in it, hung food and water dishes off the metal mesh in front, and put Dorian in it at bedtime, setting it on top of Al's dresser so the bird could easily see us and realize how close we were. We covered all but the front of it with a small blanket so he could have a nice, dark cave of his own but still see that we were nearby.

Dorian's sleeping box

That did the trick, and he quickly learned to sleep there. He does to this day, though after a few years we weaned him out of our bedroom. He's now quite happy to go to bed in his "sleepy box" which resides in our living room. The reason we moved him out of the bedroom will become apparent in a later section entitled "Sunrise is the Time to Wake Up - Birdy Alarm Clock".

GROWING UP IS HARD TO DO (ESPECIALLY ON US!)

or

"Doctor, How Do I Interact With My Parrot Without Losing Blood?"

Earlier, I mentioned that when Dorian was a baby he was very protective of Al. This close relationship carried with it an intrinsic problem: me. The bird was aware that there was a close relationship between Al and me and he was possessively jealous. The result was that every time I tried to get near Al or the bird I'd get seriously bitten. As the behaviorist we consulted described it, "Dorian only wants one thing from Dru – that she folds up and dies." This most certainly would not do – not only was I unable to have a relationship with the young parrot, any time I approached my husband it elicited squawks, whistles, and other protestation, up to and including the drawing of my blood. We sort of just "put up" with this for about three years, and then something inevitable happened: Dorian matured into an adult.

Little did we know that when Greys become adults they VIOLENTLY reject their mothers. I'm sure this is an excellent strategy to maintain species diversity but it came as a shock and a heartbreak to Al. Suddenly his sweet, adoring baby wanted to draw HIS blood.

At the same time I suddenly became Dorian's love interest. I can't image why; I never once sent him flowers or asked him to a movie, but – yes - the bird went from wanting me to curl up and die to wanting me to accept his courting advances and run away to build a little nest together someplace. I pointed out to him that old adage that "a fish may love a bird but where would they build a home?" but he didn't pay attention. Suddenly I was the best thing since sliced kiwis and M&Ms and Al had been relegated to the position of "chew toy".

This was terrible from both Al's and my points of view. On the one hand, I never wanted to be the center of Dorian's universe, and frankly, his courtship behavior was (and still is) less than enchanting. You see, when Greys court a mate, they do so by offering them food. Oh, not nice, fresh food (can you imagine Dorian picking up a cookie and dropping it in my hand? Hah! No such luck). Greys, who are known to mate year round, regurgitate mostly digested food for their prospective beloved,

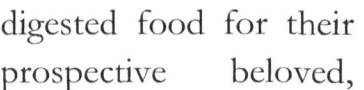
Hah! I only WISH he'd offer me FLOWERS!!

and if you've never abruptly found a milky pile of loose oatmeal on your hand, why, you just haven't LIVED!

To this day, when he goes into mating behavior he attempts to give me predigested gifts, which I try with all my heart to discourage. He ends up re-swallowing it himself but he doesn't give up. He also puffs out his feathers and gets all sorts of excited; chuffing and puffing and nearly hyperventilating to the point that I sometimes fear he's going to pass out. Thankfully, these episodes only last for a few days at a time.

Well, let's get back to the more important part of our problem with his maturation: his rejection of Al. Now HE couldn't approach the bird without getting bitten to the point of drawn blood, so our roles were now entirely reversed. This could NOT go on so we consulted the bird behaviorist again, who spent several hours enlightening us and giving us guidance as to how to overcome this natural but entirely unacceptable turn of events. For the most part, the strategy she outlined worked, though Dorian is still apt to bite without warning (like he did just this morning when Al was petting him.) Here's what we did:

Since Dorian now had a vested interest in pleasing me (his potential mate) we focused on and used that proclivity. I would hand Dorian to Al and keep a close eye on him, telling him to be nice and behave himself. All I wanted at that point was for Al to hold the bird without getting bitten and all

Dorian wanted was to please me, so just as I watched HIM closely, Dorian watched ME closely, as though to say, "Do you see me being nice to the icky, nasty dirt-ball? Aren't I wonderful? Don't you just love me for being so nice to him?"

Over time this worked to break the ice and Dorie's relationship with Al improved, though it will never be as close as it once was, which is a terrible pity. Al will never be able to entirely trust Dorian again – and with good reason. That's something owners of birds need to be aware of. **Sometimes the bird will choose one owner to shower affection on while they abuse or ignore another.**

This brings me to another interesting and important issue about our little "Il Duce"…

DORIAN'S RELATIONSHIP WITH EACH OF US

It's clear to see that Dorian has a different relationship with each of us. As mentioned above, at first I was The-Evil-Interloper-Who-Wants-Mommy-Bird's-Attention. As Dorian matured, however, I became Darling-Mate-and-Preener-Slave.

Al began as Dear-Darling-Mommy-Feeder-and-Protector and ended up as "Him-Over-There-Who-I-Put-Up-With-Only-So-Dru-Will-Still-Like-Me. At the same time, whenever he becomes frightened or terribly hungry, he'll go to Al for safety and food. It should be noted that while at dinner time we feed the birds some of the same food we're eating, it always tastes better if Dorian eats it off Al's plate.

When we first obtained Dorian our daughter Rachael was 16 years old, and from the first, she was his designated Playmate. He allows her to handle him in ways he won't let either Al or me attempt. She can do "bird tipping"; her equivalent of "cow tipping", where she holds Dorian on her hand and just tips him over onto his side (usually onto her leg). He won't let us do that. She can hug and cuddle him against her chest and murmur onto the top of his head, to which he'll reply with a similar growly sound, and she can lean in and kiss him under his wings, or blow the dander powder out from under them; activities he'd never allow us to attempt.

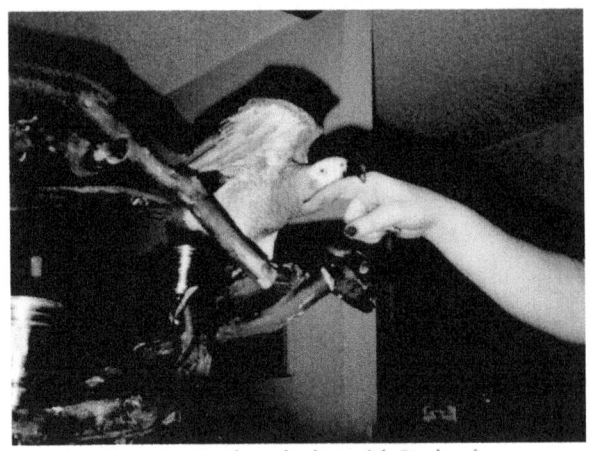
Dorian playing with Rachael

In the photo to the left Dorian is playing with Rachael and has taken hold of her finger. Though parrots' beaks are capable of inflicting extreme damage, he's just holding and not putting pressure on her finger. Amazing, isn't it?

Like all prey animals, Dorian is cautious and fearful of strangers, with some odd exceptions. Whenever we have company that stays for more than a few minutes Dorian becomes curious about who these people are and often asks to come out of his cage to look them over. We allow this, putting him on a T-stand or playpen at a distance from our guests, and making sure one of us (usually me) is situated strategically between the bird and the visitors. For the most part Dorian stays where he's put (unless I've put some nice food snacks on the table) but once in a while a guest will have that "je ne sais quoi" that attracts the bird as though they were covered in apples and sunflower seeds. In these cases, despite all admonitions to the contrary, he'll fly, leap, or waddle over to this person to look at him closely (it's mostly men he's drawn to) and sometimes he'll actually want to climb up onto them (which I very rarely allow lest he decide to bite) and he'll often put his head down near these favored persons to solicit scratches and petting.

To this day I have no idea what it is about these people that so attracts him.

THE DAILY ROUTINE

Over the years we fell into a fairly consistent regimen.

For several years my work schedule required me to rise at 5:00am, so I was always the first of the "flock" to awaken. After washing and dressing I would awaken Dorian and put him on a T-Stand for his morning "potty".

Many bird species hold their droppings until the morning and when they finally "let go" it can be seriously prodigious. Because of this I always hurried to ensure Dorie relieved himself in the appropriate place. Believe me, cleaning that much bird-poo off a carpet is enough to make you late for work even if you work from home!

Once this important task was done we went downstairs where I permitted him to wander where he would while I prepared breakfast and fresh water for all the birds. At this time I also prepared the stuff Al would need to get him off to work (you know – coffee, vitamins, shoes, that sort of thing).

During this time Dorian would generally go into our guest bathroom where he delighted in climbing up the bookshelf and shredding the out-of-date magazines I put there for his amusement. My imagination tells me he was building nests because he clearly became very upset every time I swept up and threw out all those tiny shreds.

I left for my office shortly before six every morning and Al (and for several years, our daughter Rachael) followed me downstairs somewhat later. One of the things they would do when Dorian was still a bappy was turn the television on to the Public TV station so the birds would be exposed to Sesame Street and other educational programs. We felt this would serve to not only keep the birds amused and interested but the humans appearing and speaking on the TV would be reassuring, and - who knew? – they might pick up some interesting words and concepts.

This turned out to be a mistake. You see, when Dorian is learning words, he starts with babbling, much like a child who must be corrected until he gets each word right. We eventually stopped leaving the television on because Dorian started babbling things we couldn't figure out, and certainly couldn't predict that whatever words he was attempting to say would be repeated in a way that would assist him in pronouncing them correctly.

I was usually the first one home and was welcomed loudly by the flock. I had a little time to myself (about enough to put down my briefcase and take off my shoes) before it was time to start dinner. As we explain in a later chapter, eating is a VERY social event and all the birds always expect to receive their share of whatever we're having for dinner. Plus, if we dine out we always take home a "birdy-bag" of leftovers to share with the hungry flock.

Oh, and in case you think "eating like a bird" means consuming tiny morsels of nearly nothing, think again. My birds chow down with an appetite that would make any mother proud. If they especially like a particular food they'll glomp it down and fill their crops with it as though it was their last meal. (A bird's crop is an expandable muscular pouch in their throat where they store food).

Dorian is privileged to eat off our plates; something we've

Dorian has an especial liking for grits (corn meal porridge) and will take a goodly share of it at any opportunity.

been allowing since he was a baby bird. In fact, during his "bappy-hood" we often took him with us to our favorite sushi bar. There he would quietly explore what was on our plates, as well as the plates of patrons sitting near us. At the time, he was very cute with his big, black baby-eyes. Maybe that explains why other patrons thought it was a story worth telling the kids back home to let him steal a piece of fish or octopus off their plates without protesting.

The point however, is that if he's particularly hungry he can eat more than a quarter of your average hamburger, perhaps a quarter cup of mashed potatoes, ENDLESS chicken bones (all my birds would fight you beak and claw for chicken bones!) and maybe a third of a cup of ice cream. For a creature 12 inches long, that's a lot of food!

After dinner was play time, during which Dorie might stay with us for scratching and preening or wander up onto the stairs to play "Watch Bird" (the stairs overlooked the front door) while he happily chewed up the carpet. Yes, he'd pull little bits out of it until after several years he'd exposed the base wood along the sides of two steps. Hey, we were thankful he didn't try chewing on the wooden bannister!

Bedtime followed anon and we first covered Rover & Polgara for the night, then carried Dorian upstairs and put him into his sleepy box and covered him up, too.

This was our routine for many years until one day the bottom dropped out of our world.

CROSSING THE COUNTRY WITH THREE UNEASY BIRDS

After living in Southern California for over 20 years, the economic unpleasantness of 2008 occurred and both Al and I lost our jobs at two separate companies on the SAME DAY! Suddenly we went from a comfortable existence in an opulent Los Angeles suburb to not even scraping by on unemployment. Despite our best efforts we were unable to find jobs and eventually we had to face the reality of downsizing. We had long been ignoring the absurdity of two people (and three birds) living in a five bedroom house but the time to sell out and downsize had come at last. We chose a new home, all the way across the country and now had to figure out how to move ourselves and our feathered companions 2500 miles from the west coast to the east.

Driving across in a car was simply out of the question. Three birds in the back of one car for that long a journey? It was difficult (and noisy) enough when we took the three of them eight miles down the road to visit their vet!

Hmm. A train? A quick check informed us that trains don't allow birds at all. The end. Not happening.

The bus? Hah! – don't even think about it. Can you see the mental images? There's Al and me on the dusty side of the road with birdcages in our hands, watching the bus disappear in the distance because the other passengers made the driver kick us and our noisy birds off in Arizona someplace.

Plane? Well, of course that was possible however airlines  have very strict rules about carrying animals inside the body of the aircraft, and though they do have a special, pressurized and temperature-controlled area for the transport of pets, this was unacceptable to us, since all we could see was our three PREY ANIMAL pets in separate kennel cabs being taken by total strangers to a strange, loud place containing PREDATORS. Birds aren't equipped to understand the fact that other animals in cages are not able to eat them, or that their own cages would protect them. Also, a lot of fear reactions in birds are autonomic – if they hear a loud noise or see sudden movement toward them their bodies will put them into panic mode – they can't help it. Now imagine them in this environment for five or six hours. Death by heart attack is a very real possibility. Now, some airlines will allow a small caged animal into the cabin with you if it's under your seat but then again, we're two humans with three birds, and even if we bought an additional seat the airlines have limits on how many animals of any kind they can allow into the cabin so there would be no guarantee that we'd be able to bring all three into this somewhat more reassuring (because we'd be right there) but still stressful environment. It also occurred to us that if any of the birds decided they simply HAD to protest vocally, the other passengers would (rightfully) complain and we could envision the pilot making a special stop somewhere to kick us off the plane. Nope, an airplane wouldn't do, either.

This left us one choice and actually it involved something Al and I had been thinking about for many years. An RV. This was the answer; a small home on wheels where we could keep the birds close to one another, constantly be there with them, and limit the stress of the move.

 Digging into our dwindling savings we put a down payment on a 32 foot Winnebago C class Recreational Vehicle and prepared the area over the driver's cab to receive three cages.

Now, like many humans, birds do NOT take to change very happily, and after living in nice, spacious cages in our large, roomy Family Room for so many years, the birds were decidedly unhappy to find themselves in these relatively tiny cages in this miniscule (in comparison) house. Well, I must point out that the day we put them into the RV had been a terribly stressful day for them anyway, with a team of movers making noise all day long and pulling our possessions out of the house. They watched the entire process with what can only be described as avian horror. By the time I gently removed each of them into their travel cages they were so emotionally worn out that they entered the cages quite readily; a fact that absolutely floored me. Moving them into the new but very quiet RV was a relief to them; especially since their cages were right next to each other.

We took our time to cross the country, only driving a few hours every day and making sure we gave the birds some time out of the small cages every day. They were clearly traumatized by these major changes and clung to us and each other for reassurance. Rover and Polgara had already endured a change of home when we originally adopted them but our Los Angeles house was the only home Dorian had ever known. Because of this, his prolonged stay in this weird, tiny, noisy, moving place was very upsetting to him, and he demanded a great deal of our attention. When we weren't petting him or talking to him, he was peeping unhappily right above our heads. It was our original intention to have all three birds sleep in their travel cages however Dorian was extremely anxious and unhappy by the end of every day and couldn't rest. Luckily I had brought his "sleepy box" with us and we found that this familiar sanctuary was a great relief to him (and us) so we put him in it every night.

Now, some people would probably scoff at our going through all this trouble and expense. They might ask, "why take over two weeks to get from here to there, and put out the money to buy the RV and fill it with gas every day just to pander to and pamper three birds? A plane trip's only 5 or 6 hours!" I'd bet that those people own dogs or cats. All I can suggest is that maybe "bird people" are a little different (crazier?). We tend to bend over backward for our companion birds for some reason. Yes, some people give their dogs and cats "people food" but not many come home from dining out and start cooking JUST for their birds. Maybe we *are* a little crazy. Maybe we used to be birds in former lives? Who can say? It's just the way it is.

GETTING USED TO THE NEW PLACE

Seventeen days after we left California we reached our final destination and parked the Winnebago in an RV park for two weeks until the closing on our new home.

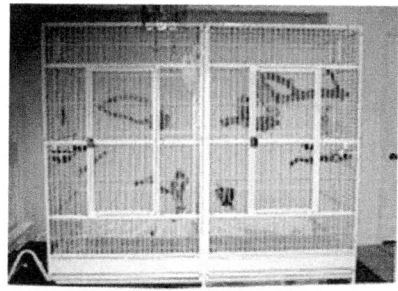
Rover & Polgara's huge, new cage

We purchased new, even larger cages for the birds and though they were clearly delighted to get out of the travel cages it took them several weeks to accept that this new place was now their home and that the new view out the window was going to be their view from now on.

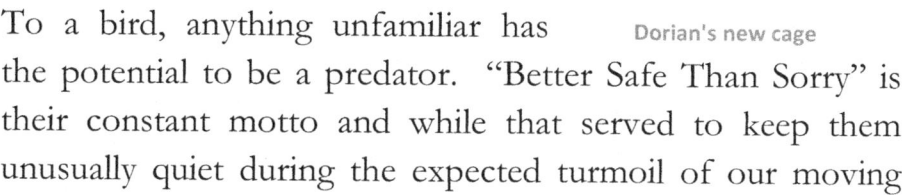
Dorian's new cage

Even Dorian, who is used to more "out-of-cage" time than the others (who eat walls, curtains, and furniture if unattended) took several weeks before he felt confident enough to want to actually explore the new house.

To a bird, anything unfamiliar has the potential to be a predator. "Better Safe Than Sorry" is their constant motto and while that served to keep them unusually quiet during the expected turmoil of our moving into the new house, it can be a little trying when you really want Dorian to stand on the brand new, huge, shiny playpen you've just dropped a hundred buck on and he looks at it as though you're pushing him toward the open mouth of a tiger. Yes, it takes birds a number of days to get used to anything new. The actual number of days varies from bird to bird, just as it takes different people different amounts of time to become comfortable in a new place or situation.

During the first weeks of our residency the birds were so quiet they wouldn't even perform their morning and evening announcement of their presence in the neighborhood. Our hopes that they might give up that habit forever were eventually dashed and now they've acclimated; probably better than we have to this new place, new climate and new way of living.

Our new daily routine established itself after a while – I usually wake up first (though thankfully no longer at 5:00am!) and once I'm dressed I wake Al, then take Dorian out of his sleepy-box and put him on the new play stand for his morning potty (yes, he finally accepted it). While he's thinking about performing this task I uncover Rover & Polgara's big cage, then go about feeding all three of them. Shortly after they've eaten (read this as 'shortly after Dorian eats his favorite bits then realizes there's no people-food or treats in his breakfast bowl') Dorie will start to call for attention. It's very important to him to spend time with Al and me since we're his favorites. The morning "imperative" is further explained in a section called "Morning is Flock Time".

After spending the majority of the morning in the company of Al and me (he doesn't necessarily require direct attention or petting or preening – just being with us is often enough) Dorian's ready to go back to his cage for an "Elevensies" snack and some quiet play-time. At this point the two other birds, who have been playing or arguing with each other all morning, also show renewed interest in their food bowls.

A peaceful hour or two of play, snacking, and preening will bring them all to nap time, which is also a daily occurrence.

Suddenly it will be five p.m., which is suppertime. No matter what Al's and my personal plans are, when it becomes five o'clock all three of our birds will start to vocalize and stand on or in front of their food dishes. I swear, if they had fingers and thumbs they'd be holding knives and forks and looking expectantly at me, as if to say, "Well? Where is it? I'm hungry NOW!"

If we're dining at home they know they'll get their share of whatever it is, though they often continue to verbally complain while I'm cooking. My assurances that it'll be ready soon apparently falls on deaf ears (yes, of course birds have ears. They're hidden under tiny feathers on the sides of their heads). If we go out to dine they have to wait until we return; at which point we will have brought them leftovers in a "birdy-bag" or I'll microwave a potato for them, which they love, as long as there's a bit of butter on it. Yes, they much prefer warm food for supper and will sometimes distain any leftovers I've taken out of the refrigerator.

After dinner it's play time until bedtime arrives. The hour of bedtime varies with the seasons, because for birds, sundown is the time to settle down. The window our birds look out of faces southwest so they get a lovely view of sunset every evening. The problem with this is that the sight of sunset alarms them and they fuss and jump around uneasily until I close the curtains so they can't see outside. I cover my birds every evening and they interpret this not only as security but as the absolute Bird Rule of Life that it's time to be quiet and find a good place to roost. No matter how much fuss they've been making, when we cover them, it's Lights Out and they immediately settle down.

There are exceptions to this last rule – during the evening if Al or I comment on or laugh at something we're seeing on the TV Dorian will also comment (mostly unintelligibly) or laugh along with us. Rover and Pol will sometimes fuss at one another after they're covered which can lead to a verbal altercation, or in the worst case, a physical altercation, leading to our separating them into the two halves of their cage. In other words, they're in bed but not necessarily asleep. Just like human kids, right?

WHY "DORIE THE DUCK"?

We often call Dorian "Dorie the Duck" or "Ducky", and he himself frequently says, "Duck-Bird" or "Hello, Ducky", and recognizes the word as an endearment.

Well, it's this way. Al and I love movies; especially science fiction and fantasy stories. 1986 saw the release of a fairly silly science fiction movie called "Howard the Duck", based on a Marvel Comics character about a civilized duck from another world who is pulled to human-dominated Earth. In the movie, Howard saves the world from an alien invasion and at the end of the story Beverly (played by Lea Thompson), the heroine-cum-rock-singer performs a song called "Howard the Duck".

Dorian's not terribly interested in movies or television but for some reason only he knows (and we've asked but he's not telling) he was fascinated by the bird-like character on the screen and leaned forward as though ready to fly to the TV during much of the film. He also apparently enjoyed the song so much that we naturally (well, sort of naturally) started singing along, substituting Dorian's name for Howard's. Thus was born "Dorie the Duck."

PART TWO – CARE, FEEDING, AND REQUIRED DAILY ABJECT WORSHIPPING

Or

HEAD DOWN – TAIL UP!**

** The normal position for ever-hungry African Greys is with their head down in a food bowl which of necessity puts their red tails up into the air. Maybe it's a signal to other Greys that there's food to be had!

BASIC CHARACTERISTICS OF THE AFRICAN GREY PARROT

Okay, let's take an overview of a typical Congo African Grey. He's a medium-sized parrot between ten and 13 inches from head to tail, with dark grey feathers on the wings, neck and back, becoming lighter on his legs and the top of his head. His eyes, which are entirely black when the bird is very young, develop into a black iris surrounded by a light grey pupil. The tiny feathers around his eyes are very light grey – nearly white and surround the eye in a lovely almond shape. His beak is entirely black.

Very young Dorian. See that his eyes are all black!

The most startling physical feature of the African Grey is his beautiful and bright red tail feathers. Overall they are beautiful creatures and – don't kid yourself – they KNOW how pretty they are!

There are two types of African Grey parrot: the Congo and the Timneh, the latter being indigenous to a more northerly part of the African continent and being somewhat smaller and lighter in color than its southern cousin, the Congo. The lifespan of Greys is in constant contention, ranging from forty years to ninety and everywhere in between. They become adult at three years of age, and according to some sources, hit middle age somewhere in their 20s. As I write this, Dorian has just turned 19 years old so I can't personally vouch for the accuracy of that estimation. I have no idea when they become "geriatric". I only know that I'll get there LONG before he does.

In the wild, Greys eat fruits, nuts, seeds, leafy greens and the occasional snail but in our homes they thrive on the same sort of healthy diet we're all supposed to eat; a variety of vegetables, fruits, grains, and proteins, with fats kept to a reasonable minimum. And like us, our three birds much prefer pizza, pasta, rice, grits, and bread. Where they developed their taste for grain products I can't imagine. I've tried to visualize Dorian in the wild – busily getting a meal off a ravioli tree in the middle of Africa but the image is difficult to bring into focus…

A parrot's digestive system is different from ours – unlike humans they eliminate both liquid and solid waste simultaneously through a bodily aperture called a cloaca; and they tend to do so every ten to fifteen minutes or thereabouts. (I've noticed over the years that the frequency of "poopage" seems to increase in proportion to the price of the clothing you're wearing when the bird is standing on your knee). The exception to this is that, like many species of birds, they hold in their waste overnight. Well, so do we, don't we?

African Greys are among the most intelligent birds on Earth, which characteristic has made them very popular as pets – even the English King Henry XIII was purported to own one. They are excellent speakers and a bird behaviorist told us that they can develop the intelligence of a 5 year old human. Our own experience with Dorian would tend to agree with that, however as we've said before, we're not scientist or veterinarian, and it's been decades since our daughter was five, so our ability to carefully compare is seriously compromised.

While it's a wonderful thing that Greys could be as smart as a five year old, emotionally they only develop as much as a 2 year old human. Imagine living with someone in their "Terrible Twos" for fifty or sixty years! Our own observations about this is that yes; they want their way at all times however Dorian doesn't say "NO" even a fraction of the amount the average human child does at this stage. It's more a difference in philosophy. Please refer to a later section called "The Most Difficult Concepts to Teach a Bird."

Despite this point of contention, Greys are wonderful and loving companions, albeit very demanding of your time and attention. No, even more demanding than that. Believe me. It's not a matter of "been there – done that." It's a matter of "being there – doing that."

NOW, THIS WON'T HURT A BIT...

Of course the first thing one wants to do with any pet is introduce them to their veterinarian. Examining a bird is a more difficult process than examining a dog or cat, not only because their bodies are so much smaller but as a prey animal, a parrot will assume that this stranger wants to pick him up in order to eat him! Well, how would YOU react if you were captured by a huge predator? All three of our birds hold this conviction. There's no doubt that all companion birds do because every avian vet is well-supplied with a selection of thick, soft towels with which they carefully swaddle the bird's body. The towel not only helps protect the bird (and the vet from the bird's talons and beak), it prevents them from flapping their wings and struggling.

Vets have a special way of holding the bird; sort of an under-the-arm-like-Tweety-is-a-strangely-shaped-football while one hand gently but firmly holds the bird's head steady. The vet can now (relatively) easily check the bird over while listening to the dulcet tones of the bird's protests; whether they be loud trumpets, nervous calls, or growls. Sometimes the birds are fairly quiet, actually, which of course is a relief to everyone.

After the exam is over we have the birds' beaks, talons, and wings taken care of. This is entirely UNLIKE a human getting a facial, pedicure, and hair styling! Here's what happens:

BEAK MAINTENANCE: Psitticine beaks grow outward from the inside and the outer layers tend to chip or flake; especially if the bird plays with the metal bars of his cage. For example, Rover is convinced that if he gnaws on the bars long enough he'll work his way out and obtain clear access to the living room vertical blinds. All he really accomplishes is to wear little chips out of his beak. To minimize damage and flaking, the vet will polish the outer layers of the bird's beak. Birds generally hate this process and protest lustily.

TALON CLIPPING: Birds' talons are naturally curved, providing a good grip on perches, food bits, and your favorite shirt (the left leg of all my trousers have multiple little pulls in them from Dorian's talons. Now you know where he prefers to stand). In the wild, talons get trimmed naturally by constant exposure to tree bark, digging in the ground, and general wear and tear. When living in a cage however, a bird has limited opportunities for nature to provide a pedicure. There are special perches available that are rough and supposedly help trim down Sweetum's talons. Some birds enjoy this however all three of our birds avoid those perches – I guess they don't feel good on the bottoms of their feet.

Birds regularly clean and maintain their feet and talons, which doesn't help matters; in fact Rover's talons grow so quickly that if he doesn't get them trimmed they get so long he has difficulty unhooking them from the metal bars as he climbs around the cage. In fact, if left untrimmed, Rover's talons become so sharp that just having him jump onto our arms will draw blood!

Once in a while Dorian allows us to set him on his back so we can dull his talons with a nail file but once we're finished he immediately starts working on them to sharpen them up again. The other two birds won't even THINK about letting us put them on their backs.

Vets are well-practiced with special guillotine clippers to shorten and blunt the talons while leaving enough of them so the bird can still cling to a perch. Admittedly, it does take the birds a day or two to figure out that they can't rely on needle-sharp nails to hold them onto their perches and they do tend to lose their footing at first.

Guillotine clippers

WING CLIPPING: Birds' wings are aerodynamic marvels but rather than get very technical we'll just mention that there are three main types of flight feathers on the typical wing. The longest, which are

The Primary Flight Feathers are circled in red. **Photo courtesy of Florida Parrot Rescue**

at the outermost part of the wing are called Primaries. The next, slightly shorter feathers are called Secondaries and the smallest flight feathers; those closest to the bird's body are called Tertials Clipping a bird's wings concerns only the ten primary flight feathers. These are cut shorter, so they still allow the bird to fly horizontally (in case the cat decides to test its hunting skills on Tweetie) but not gain altitude. This prevents the bird from flying into the tree in your back yard in case you decide to take her outside with you** or head out for points south, in which case you can wave a fond farewell as she disappears forever.

** We recommend against taking a companion bird outside unless it's in an aviary or carrying conveyance. Predators ARE everywhere and we've heard of birds being snatched off their owner's shoulder by hawks or owls! Always be on the alert!

There are other venues that offer beak, nail and wing maintenance such as pet stores and private groomers however since birds should be examined yearly anyway, why not kill two…uh, never mind…your vet can take care of it all in one visit. They do tend to be more expensive than pet stores or groomers though, so the choice is really up to you.

Another caveat you need to consider is the expertise of the groomer. We had one experience where the person we hired to do a "house call" to trim our birds had been in the industry of selling birds, cages, and supplies for many years, and had been offering trimming services for as long. Upon  hearing of her reputation we felt pretty confident in her abilities so we called her up and made an appointment. She came to our house with an assistant and they started with Polgara's talons while I looked on like an anxious "mommy bird". The first thing I noticed was that the woman was not using the expected guillotine clipper but a simple "human" nail clipper that you or I might use. I'd always thought that this type of clipper would tend to pinch the nail, increasing the likelihood of splintering but I didn't say anything because I figured she must know what she was doing. The next thing I noticed was that over half the clipped nails were bleeding! This "expert" was regularly cutting the nails too short! Admittedly, I had asked her to clip their talons as short as they could safely be cut but one would think a so-called "expert" would know what that meant and NOT allow so much bloodshed. In fact, after each clip she used a rough nail file to smooth out the cut and I was somewhat horrified to see blood streaking across the file! Still, fool that I was, I let this abuse continue. She seemed to do all right in wing clipping and beak polishing so I swallowed hard and looked on as she moved to the other two birds where the bloodshed continued.

Now, whenever we had taken our birds to the vet and had their wings, nails, and beaks done, the birds had been taken out of the room for these procedures so I thought perhaps it was so the owners wouldn't have to watch this disturbing blood-letting. There was one difference with this "expert", however. Usually, after returning home from the vet's office, all three birds would be sort of subdued and quiet for an hour or two, then would return to their normal activities, with the exception of having to get used to the shorter talons and the now-limited ability to fly. After being handled by this groomer however, all three of my birds stopped eating for the rest of the day, held one foot up for three days, and moved as little as possible. This "expert" had hurt my birds! I can't say whether she pinched toes or nails, or the too-short nails themselves were hurting but for a few days none of them wanted to move much at all. In fact, one behavior the birds were used to doing after a nail trimming was to immediately start their own grooming process on their nails. After this incident none of the birds would touch their own feet for about three days. The moral of this awful story is to be really, really sure of your experts — if you can't watch the actual procedure, watch the behavior of the bird afterward! CAVEAT EMPTOR! ("Let the Buyer Beware!")

There's a reason we allow the vet to perform the beak, talon, and wing maintenance for us. Birds tend to associate unpleasant experiences with the person who made it happen. We'd rather our birds think the vet is the bad guy. Keeps us on better terms with the flock!

Oh, one more thing you shouldn't overlook. Whenever you take birds to their avian vet you should use a small carrier or travel cage to transport them even if you know they won't fly away from you. If there's a nice, big dog in the waiting room the bird will feel much safer with the walls of a cage around him!

How do you find a good avian vet? The Association of Avian Veterinarians has a wonderful website that will assist you in finding an avian vet in your area. (http://www.aav.org/)

PROVIDING A PROPER BIRD HOME

It's always important to keep in mind that birds are prey animals – therefore not at all like dogs or cats or people. If they're going to stay healthy and happy they need to be part of a flock, which implies not being isolated from other family members. For birds, there is comfort in numbers.

They also need a refuge; a space to call their own where they feel safe. This, of course, would be their cage. The overall rule of thumb about cages is "the bigger the better". A cage that will not even allow a bird to stretch out his wings can make the bird claustrophobic, and it might develop stress behaviors such as screaming, feather-plucking or self-mutilation (more about these behaviors in a later section called "Traumatic Behavior"). There are general guidelines available on the internet, through vets and reputable pet stores as to how big, or at least what the minimum recommended size would be for a bird cage, depending on the size of the bird and the number of birds who will share the cage. Not only the overall size of the cage but the distance between the bars and the thickness of the bars is something to be considered. Too wide bar spacing will encourage a bird to try to squeeze out of the cage and a bird stuck between the bars is NOT something you want to deal with! Too thin a bar is an invitation to a larger bird (like our cockatoo) to bite through it and happily make its way out of the cage. If you're not home when this Houdini escaping act occurs I don't even want to THINK about the destruction a bird with a large beak can wreak on the tasty furniture, walls, curtains, and handmade tablecloth your Aunt Mildred took four years to stitch for you.

For a bird the size of an African Grey Parrot, the minimum sized cage should be about 24"x 36"x 48" with bars spaced at ¾ to about an inch apart. Most cages come with only one or two perches; generally of a cheap, soft wood. Keep in mind that birds, not having hands, play with their mouths, and in the wild they derive some amount of nutrition and beak maintenance from chewing on the trees in which they perch.

Rover the Cockatoo has been working on the above perch for a few weeks.

Soft wood perches will eventually be chewed through. Hardwood perches are available through many sources such as pet stores, online, and I found a good source at my local farmer's market. Manzanita, dragon wood, and java wood are all dense enough to stand up to constant bird munching; at least for a decent amount of time.

Now think about where birds live. Trees don't consist of two or three uniformly spaced, perfectly cylindrical perches – they're chock full of branches of all sizes facing in every possible direction. I've been told that not providing enough perches is the number one "decorating mistake" owners make when creating a home for their birds. I don't mean one should put so much wood in the cage that the bird can't jump around or extend its wings – just enough to make moving within it interesting and varied.

Some of the perches in Rover and Polgara's big cage. You can see Rover on the bottom left – his crest raised in suspicion of the camera.

Oh, one more detail about perches. Birds feel safer the higher up they're able to go in the cage. Putting at least one perch up near the top of the cage (though not so high that the bird has to crouch down to stand on it) will provide a refuge for Downy-Dumpling in case the neighbor comes to visit and brings his Golden Retriever.

Naturally, the bottom of the cage must be lined to catch food and droppings. Plain, black and white newspaper is fine for this, or plain shipping paper. Antimicrobial lining paper is also available however it's obviously more costly than the other two options. By the way, colored newsprint or glossy magazine pages should be avoided, since the inks may be toxic and you can be guaranteed that "Chirpy-Burpy" will spend some quality time reaching down to retrieve that paper so he can chew on it, pull it up through the grating, and generally use it to redecorate his cage.

Here's another thought. If the birds are going to sleep in the cage they'll be happiest if you provide at least one of the following: A perch high up (as previously mentioned), a box or covered area in which they can feel protected (though it's a guarantee that they'll chew on that, too), or a dark-colored cover to put over the entire cage every evening.

As we've related, Dorian sleeps in a Kennel Cab every night which we've provided with a few perches, a small ladder, and a toy or two. We cover this each evening with a small lap blanket. Our two other birds live together in a huge cage that we cover every evening with a piece of felt 72" wide and 4 yards long so it covers the top and the two long sides of their cage. We also put dark bath towels over the ends of the cage, though Rover delights in pulling them down and trying to work them into the cage so he can make caves and nests of out them. This, by the way, means the towels become his toys and eventually he'll chew them into rags. He also chews on the main cover but it takes him over a year to bring it to the point that it has to be replaced. That's why we don't buy expensive bird covers. Just so you know. Rover is the only one of our three birds who does this, by the way. It's a matter of personal taste. Some birds chew their covers – some don't.

Putting the cover on their cage signals to Rover and Polgara that it's time to settle down for the night and they follow this rule pretty consistently. In the morning we'll likely find them cuddling together on one of the two highest perches we've installed for them.

Keep in mind that even the largest, gilded cage is still a cage and all birds need some time without bars around them. We have two T-Stands and a bird playpen we use to give our flock some interesting "out" time. These times MUST be supervised, as their natural curiosity and belief that they own everything will prompt the birds to see if they can pull nesting material out of that 200 year old tapestry you inherited from Rich Uncle Edgar. If they leave that alone they might fly across the room instead to helpfully remove those ugly pearls and sequins on the blouse you had hanging up before packing it to go to the wedding.

A bird playpen or play gym is the perfect place to allow "Snookums" some space to spread his wings. They should be hung with toys of his favorite kinds plus food and water and enough places to walk or climb around on to keep him amused and happy. How long should a bird be permitted to stay on the playpen? As long as you can happily keep an eye on him, or until you decide (or he decides) it's time to go back to the cage. Playpen time is also a good time to interact directly with the bird, playing games, talking, singing, petting, and generally having fun together.

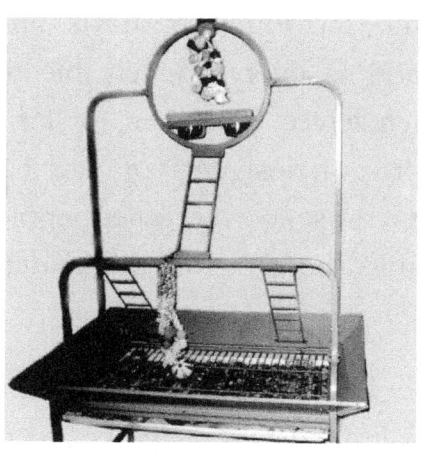

CLEANING THE CAGE, THE PLAYPEN, THE FLOOR, AND YOURSELF

One of the major downsides to living with birds is the mess they make. Keeping their environment clean is probably the most important way to keep birds healthy, as discarded bits of food and dried droppings can attract bacteria, mold, insects, and even rodents (mice LOVE bird food)!

As mentioned in the introduction, birds are notoriously messy and throw food in every conceivable direction. As well, they relieve themselves every ten or 15 minutes, and despite the best efforts of designers of bird cages and bird play gyms, somehow those clever little bappies figure out how to poop right onto the rungs of the ladders they use to climb up and down.

Seed catchers at the bottom of cages and play gyms are helpful but only in a limited way. I've yet to meet the bird who can't easily toss leftovers well beyond the rim of the widest seed catcher. That's not to say they're useless; they do deflect a percentage of the mess inward to the bottom of the cage however one should never expect them to save you a whole lot of vacuuming or wall washing time.

DAILY CLEANING

Birds' food and water dishes must be washed with hot water and soap every day. Obviously leftover food must be removed but even if the water looks pristine, it must be discarded and the water bowl washed. Dorian tends to keep his water looking clean but when he takes a drink he dips his tongue into the water, thus depositing any bits of food or shreds of toys etc., and this can build up a bacterial growth faster than you'd think.

Today's water with bits of food and Rover's molted feathers

Rover and Polgara like to dip their food into their water so it's a daily surprise to see whether we'll find a soggy piece of bread, an inadvertently dropped banana chip, or the water itself an exciting shade of whatever colored wooden toy has been dropped into it.

Oh, and Rover, always an innovator, likes putting his toys into his food bowls. Here is a picture of today's donation – a bit of blue rope toy that was originally meant for a dog. It had a tennis ball on either end however Rover chewed those into tiny bits less than a week after we gave him the toy.

If you keep a birdbath in the cage there's no doubt it will need to be cleaned every day in the same way you clean the food and water dishes.

Since birds don't plan ahead or understand the consequences of pooping on their perches or toys, these should be checked every day, and any poopage should be removed so they're not standing in or playing with their own droppings (just the thought of that is fairly yucky). I certainly don't want Dorian standing on me after he's had a stroll through some nice, sticky poop!

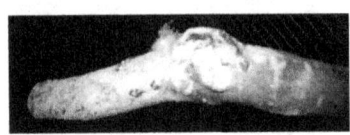

Plentifully pooped-on perch

The paper at the bottom of the cage should be changed every day to avoid bacterial growth or invasion by insects. I admit that I'm guilty of letting it go for longer periods of time but once the corners of the cage where the food bowls are located start to collect leftovers that I really don't want the birds to reach for and nibble on I relent, go grab a pair of disposable latex gloves, and get to it.

While not the most pleasant activity I can think of (it doesn't even make my list of top 100 things I like to do), changing the paper at the bottom of the cages, T-stands, and play gym isn't really difficult or too time-consuming. Get a large trash bag ready, pull out the bottom tray of the cage and fold up the newspaper or whatever lining material you're using and take it directly from the tray to the trash bag. Now, in nearly 25 years of cleaning bird cages I've never once been able to do that without some amount of food scraps escaping, so I also keep handy a whisk broom and dust pan to collect those bits. Oh, and don't be awfully disappointed to find amongst this trash the succulent lychee nut (or other treat) that you had especially imported from China (or wherever) at an unbelievably exorbitant price with only one bite taken out of it. There's no accounting for tastes. On Monday "Fluffums" may have gobbled up that treat like it was his last meal, and on Tuesday he might look at it as though he's convinced you're trying to poison him. Don't take it personally. Save the bucks.

Okay, now that you've emptied the tray, don't be surprised to find that somehow they've managed to poop in exactly the right place to avoid the paper entirely and leave a nice, crusty blob here and there around the edges. No, they don't do it on purpose...I think. Just wash it with the same soap and hot water as you did the food bowls, or if you're able, take it outside and use the garden hose on it, then DRY IT COMPLETELY before you put down the new lining paper.

The grating that lives between the liner tray and the birds should also be removed and cleaned. This isn't that easy, since poopage and discarded food does accumulate on it. Take it outside and hose it down or take it into the kitchen and scrub it down. This method is more pleasant if the weather outside is forbidding but it carries the added necessity of having to clean and disinfect the kitchen after you're done.

Oh, and if you want to disinfect the grating and liner tray, please do **NOT** spray them with commercial aerosol disinfectants! Many household cleaning products that are perfectly safe around humans, cats, and dogs are VERY unhealthy to use around birds! These include (but are not limited to) any aerosol that can be inhaled such as disinfectants, air fresheners, carpet fresheners and related products. Also candle or plug-in air fresheners are bad for birds; again, the chemicals float into the air and can be inhaled. If you feel you absolutely must disinfect the cage, just use natural products, such and vinegar and water and make sure the grating and tray are absolutely dry before returning them to the cage.

Sweeping up or vacuuming the area surrounding the cage is a daily – even a more-than-once-daily priority. This not only prevents bits of food, feathers, fluff, and shreds of paper from being ground into the carpet and attracting invaders, it keeps your feet safe from harm if you happen to enjoy going barefoot around the house. We considered getting one of those robotic vacuums to continuously patrol the area but we didn't do it for two reasons: first, we thought it would terrorize the birds to have this strange THING wandering around all the time and secondly, with the amount of feathers, food and other stuff our three birds throw on a daily basis it would overfill the machine in no time flat and I'd spend the time I now spend sweeping on picking up and emptying the robot vacuum. Six of one, half a dozen of the other...

WEEKLY/MONTHLY CLEANING OF THE CAGE

Whether you clean the cage weekly or monthly depends on you, the cage, and the bird. Smaller birds such as parakeets, canaries or finches don't make that much of a mess. If you have larger birds or more than one bird the mess increases significantly and it becomes more important to clean the cage more often.

All you have to do to determine when to wash down the cage is be watchful. Pay attention. What makes you think that since the bird has successfully thrown that mouthful of spaghetti with meat sauce onto the front of your shirt that he hasn't also landed some on the bars and perches and toys in his cage? Oh, yes he has.

Dorian loves Italian food. Sometimes he even allows us to have some of the spaghetti!

Cleaning a large bird cage is a big job so it will be easier if you collect everything you need before you begin. These include disposable latex gloves, cleaning cloths, scrubbing tools such as old toothbrushes, scrubbing brushes (try to avoid the metallic ones you use on barbeques, as it will tend to damage the coating on the bars of the cage), poop remover (available at most pet stores),hot, soapy water, trash bag, and lining paper.

Now, the very first thing you should do is remove the birds. Put them on a play gym if you think they're likely to stay there or in a travel cage or whatever enclosure you use when you take them to the vet. Rover and Polgara's cage has a gate in it which we use if they're sparring and need to be separated so when cleaning their cage I just put the birds in one half while I clean the other.

Next, remove the toys and perches (if that's feasible). These items can be hand-washed or taken outside to be hosed down. If the cage itself isn't too big it also can be taken outside and washed with a garden hose. If it's too large, this must be done by reaching in and applying a goodly amount of elbow grease while practicing your contortionist exercises so you reach every corner. The cage Polgara and Rover live in is too large and heavy to be moved outside so in order to clean it I take out the grating and liner then stand INSIDE the cage to scrub everything down. (Rover and Pol think this is VERY intrusive – they're sure I'm going to move in.) The grating and liner are cleaned in the usual way (noted above). Once clean, everything can be disinfected but make sure everything's completely dry before you put the birds back. Yes, it's a big, dirty job but you know the saying…

Monthly cleaning is a good opportunity to swap out the birds' toys, by the way. Even if you've been swapping out the same sets of toys you've had for a decade the birds will enjoy the change and treat the toys as brand new and fascinating.

Many cleaning products are available at pet stores and online that are safe for use around birds and will help safely clean and sanitize the cage as well as making it easier to remove dried-on food bits and droppings without using up all your elbow-grease.

After everything else is done don't forget to vacuum the carpet (or wash the floor if it's tile or stone) beneath and around the cage.

Additional information on cleaning birdcages can be found online and through reputable stores and veterinarians.

EATING IS A SOCIAL EVENT!

The natural position of African Grey Parrots is to have their tail up in the air and their head down in a bowl of food. They are the original chow-hounds, and Dorian is no exception. Among his many culinary loves he has an inordinate fondness for just about anything dairy. Ice cream, various cheeses, and nearly anything you pour cream onto are high on his list of favorites. He'll fight you for a piece of pizza.

Now, there's an important Bird Rule that you need to be aware of: If YOU'RE eating, your bird(s) had better be invited to the party or you WILL hear about it, long and loud!!

As I've mentioned earlier, I feed all three of my birds with a healthy "pelleted" food along with a variety of nuts, chopped veggies, grains, and fruits in the mornings and leave other foods (including "people" food) for suppertime.

Tofu is yummy!

Actually, this was, in part, a lie. While it's true that I feed all the birds a healthy variety of food early every morning, by the time Al and I have our own breakfast the birds are ready for "Second

Breakfast" and often loudly DEMAND a share of whatever we're eating. For example, Dorian won't refuse a few mouthfuls of scrambled eggs. He also has a fondness for tofu, which you can see him nibbling on in the photo on the previous page.

Then there's "Elevensies." Al and I don't eat at that time but by late morning the birds are back at their bowls nibbling at whatever's still in there. I find that Rover tends to taste every bite of his pelleted food, crunching each piece into tiny tidbits, some of which he's GOT to have actually swallowed, though I can't swear to the truth of that.

Birds will snack throughout the day but at 5:00pm they know it's suppertime and the entire flock must share the food or they'll tell us ALL about it! I have no idea how they tell that it's 5 o'clock but if I'm not already in the kitchen cooking by that time they're certain to verbally tell me to get a move on – they're HUNGRY!

Like people, each of our birds has particular food preferences. For example, Polgara loves dried banana chips and will dip each piece into her water dish before nibbling on it however she won't go near fresh bananas. I suspect there's something special about banana chips because sometimes she'll pick up a piece and start whistling and peeping in the shrillest voice imaginable. In fact, you should be grateful that you can't hear it from where you are. I have no idea what the excitement is over that banana chip – maybe she's hoping Mr. Right will fly by and want to share it with her? It could happen…nah…no it couldn't.

Dorian loves apples but neither of the other birds like them. He's more fond of "people food" than the others but they take and eat their share of whatever's for supper every night. All three share a love of specific "people" foods that you might not ordinarily think of as something a bird would want. Potatoes (with butter and green peas), carrots, pizza, and pasta are great favorites, along with nearly any kind of land animal meat you can think of (they're not all that fond of anything that comes out of the sea). All birds like suet and other fats, so if invited to visit your beautifully grilled Rib Eye steak, don't be surprised if Fluffsie zeroes in on the fat even more than the meat.

They all like corn, both on and off the cob, and as mentioned earlier, Dorian loves grits (which is made from cornmeal) so much he'll leap down if he sees Al or me eating it and will hastily dig in. We always consider ourselves fortunate that he graciously leaves some for us. Peanut butter on toast is also a treat enjoyed by all the birds, though we think they have to be in the mood for it. Well, so do I, now that I think about it.

Dorian also loves ice cream, which neither of the other birds will go near. It's actually fortunate that Dorian so enjoys dairy products because African Grey Parrots have a tendency toward calcium deficiency and if he didn't like cheese and ice cream and whipped cream so much I would need to give him calcium supplements. In fact, he not only will eagerly dip his beak into whipped cream, he'll happily eat a pat of butter if permitted to do so (we learned this the hard way, and NO, it's not part of his planned diet!!).

Another excellent food many people provide their birds is referred to as "chop." This consists of a wide variety of fresh vegetables, pasta, peppers, beans, grains, dried fruits and nuts which are chopped via food processor into very small bits, mixed together thoroughly, and offered daily. There is no set recipe for chop; the ingredients are whatever fresh vegetables are available plus whatever other ingredients you wish you include. Even frozen vegetables can be included. Recipe ideas for chop are available online, and these mixtures can easily be frozen into daily meal packs. Chop provides an excellent variety of nutritious foods and often is the only way birds will eat certain foods, like broccoli (does this sound like anybody's human children?). A cautionary note: like all perishable foods, chop should be removed and discarded no longer than three hours after presenting it or it will begin to spoil.

Birds have very hearty appetites and will happy snack all day long, so any time you hear someone say they "eat like a bird" you can feel free to laugh heartily.

AN IMPORTANT NOTE ABOUT SOME PARROT FOODS:

There are excellent pelleted bird foods available at every chain pet store and many independent pet stores and vets' offices. Veterinarians are more than happy to recommend what brand and type would be best, and we took our own vet's advice about this issue. On the other side of the coin, I'm always horrified when I see certain ready-made parrot foods in grocery stores and some pet stores. These usually contain a mixture of various nuts and dried fruits but ABOUND in a huge percentage of safflower and sunflower seeds. These packages usually say something appealing, like "Your bird will LOVE this".

Yeah, it will because nuts and seeds (especially sunflower seeds) are very high in fats and the bird will probably eat them first, filling up on the seeds and ignoring the more nutritious bits. It's like seeing a package in the grocery labeled "Your Child Will Love This!" and finding chocolate bars, lollipops, fruit rolls, and a few carrots and broccoli florets in the bag. Yup; guaranteed the kids will love it but what parts will they eat first, and how much nutrition are they going to get?

A varied, balanced diet is best for your bird, just like it's best for you and your human family. Following this simple philosophy allowed our male parakeet to live for 17 years, when the average lifespan of these birds is ten years! Seeds should be kept to a minimum and only used as treats or as a training reward.

Since birds don't like anything in their lives to change, new foods are best accepted when they're introduced gradually as part of their existing diet. If you've gotten a wonderful deal on a twenty pound bag of "Yummy-Gazummy Birdie Nummies" and can't wait to share this treasure with dear, little "Rodan", don't just empty everything else out of the food cup and pour this new food in. Rodan will eye that bowl like it contained a quiver of cobras! New foods need to be added gradually, at first as a small part of their regular diet, and gradually increased over several days. If you're lucky, it'll be accepted. If Rodan doesn't like it you might as well try giving it to the neighbor's dog.

Despite the best efforts of vets and bird food manufacturers, what birds want most is PEOPLE FOOD. And they can eat it happily, with a few major exceptions:

HOW TO POISON A PARROT

For the most part one can plan a parrot's diet to be much like our own: providing proteins and carbs, limiting the intake of fats, making sure the bird gets proper exercise – you know – the same drill you more or less ignore for your OWN health. Birds enjoy a great number of the same foods we like to eat, with a few exceptions that are toxic to them.

One item in particular that is highly toxic to Psitticines is AVOCADOS, which contain a fungicidal toxin called "persin", the ingestion of which can quickly lead to cardiac arrest and death. **NEVER LET YOUR BIRD NEAR GUACAMOLE OR ANYTHING WITH AVOCADOS IN IT.**

 Other foods that are toxic are rhubarb (which contains oxalic acid), apple and pear seeds, and the pits of cherries, peaches, and apricots. These contain cyanide. Caffeine and alcohol are also dangerous and must be avoided.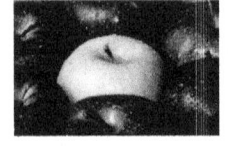

Raw dried beans also contain a poison called hemaglutin, so while cooked beans are very nutritious, avoid feeding raw beans to birds.

Also, the leaves, stems and vines of the tomato plant are toxic, being in the nightshade family, though the fruit itself is safe.

I've heard and read through several sources that chocolate is also not good for parrots. It's also not good for dogs or cats, or if it comes right down to it, it's probably just as bad for us as it is for them. There's caffeine in it among other things and yet we all still love it; Dorian included.  With this knowledge in mind I try to minimize the amount I allow him. Wish I had that much control for myself, actually.

We also learned (the hard way) that Dorian is allergic to Kimchee; a spicy Korean dish made primarily of fermented Napa Cabbage and other vegetables. We shared a bit with him and he suddenly couldn't stop scratching himself, to the point that we had to rush him to the first veterinarian who was open after 6pm and get him a shot. Several subsequent days of medicating the bird (no easy task!) got him through the worst of it. Since we didn't offer the kimchee to the other birds I have no idea if they too would be allergic to it but the lesson is that food allergies CAN exist in birds, so BE CAREFUL!

Other, NON-FOOD toxins that should be mentioned are as follows:.

Teflon and other non-stick cooking materials can emit toxic particles and gasses if overheated. An article online from

Environmental Working Group (read the article at

 http://www.ewg.org/reports/toxicteflon) notes that at 464 degrees harmful particles are released, and at 680 degrees harmful gasses are emitted. Worse, it only takes about three and a half minutes for an unattended pan to reach over 700 degrees!

NEVER leave a non-stick pan unattended or empty on a hot cooking surface!

Many aerosol spray and cleaning products could be fatal if a bird inhales the fumes. The Caged Bird Courier has an excellent list of such items, accessible online at: http://yourparrotcage.com/Bird%20Care/Toxic%20to%20your%20Bird.html

For those who do not access the internet, a synopsized listing of these substances is below:

Aerosol sprays
Chlorine & other bleaches
Hair dyes or treatments
Household cleaning products
Matches
Nail Polish
Paint & paint remover

Air or carpet fresheners
Cigarette smoke
Hair spray
Indelible markers
Mothballs
Nail polish remover
Pesticides

WHY DORIAN HAS NEVER LEARNED TO SAY "EXCUSE ME"

Birds don't generally burp so don't EVER give them anything carbonated. I've read anecdotes from veterinarians who believe they MAY be ABLE to burp but there's apparently been no research or recording of such a thing, though I have read another article in which a parakeet was fed champagne and died shortly thereafter; possibly from a burst stomach.

The closest thing we've ever heard Dorian do is imitate OUR burping but even then he doesn't seem to have any idea what it really is. In fact, whenever Dorian hears a soda can being opened he makes a burp sound!

As to flatulating, the scientific jury still seems to be out on that issue as well. Some say they're able and others argue against. Personally, I've never heard any of my birds do either, and that's all I can really say on the issue.

Since the questions have never been answered, the simple logic tells me that, no matter how tempting your carbonated beverage may look, do NOT offer it to a bird. Better safe than sorry!

BIRD ETIQUETTE – RULES THE FLOCK MUST FOLLOW (THIS INCLUDES YOU)

Anything New in the Environment Wants To Eat You

Much like the motto of private pilots, the motto of birds says, "There are Old Birds and Bold Birds, but never Old, Bold Birds." (note that even the bold, animated birds that feel compelled to take revenge on pigs are NOT long-lived!)

Rule Number One in the bird world (and I would surmise it's the number one rule for *all* prey animals) is that anything unfamiliar to you, whether moving or not, has a high probability of wanting to eat you.

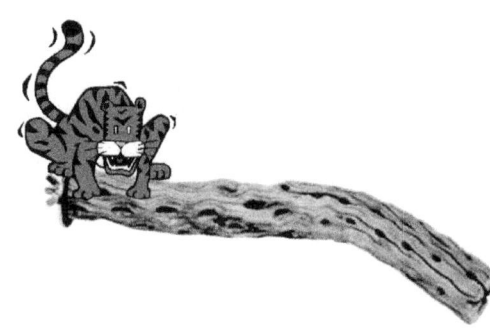

It might LOOK exactly like the perch you just ate through yesterday but…YOU NEVER KNOW. Best to wait a day or two before coming within two feet of it. The length of time it takes a bird to approach something new is directly proportional to how much you paid for it multiplied by how badly you need the bird to start using it.

Eating is Social

This is such a basic and important rule that an entire section of this book has been devoted to it. Look back a few pages and you'll find it.

The Bird on the Highest Perch is the BOSS

Height confers stature for an important reason – the bird highest in the tree is the flock's sentinel; the individual in the best position to alert the flock to the presence of some creature likely to attack them, be it snake or coyote or hawk.

Because of this, the bird whose head is higher up than the other birds gets to "rule the roost" and gets to GIVE the orders (such as "Run Away! A hawk is nearby!") and IGNORE orders given by anybody else.

Some vultures that perched in a neighbor's tree

This is one reason why, despite the example set by Long John Silver, you should NEVER allow a bird to sit on your shoulder. In their opinion, despite their relative size, this puts their head above yours, and the higher bird does NOT have to mind any bird whose head is lower than his.

The Bird Owns Any Place It Can Reach

There are other very important reasons never to allow a bird to perch on your shoulder. Anyplace you regularly allow the bird to go becomes, in the bird's mind, its territory. It will DEFEND its territory against any interlopers coming near – like your spouse or your child!

Controlling a bird involves eye contact – something that's nearly impossible if it's on your shoulder. It's also very hard to see and interpret a bird's body language if you can't look directly at it.

There have been many cases of people being seriously bitten in the face because they've startled, annoyed, or otherwise upset the bird on their shoulder. I myself have had my ear bitten into, and you'd be surprised by how much you can bleed from there - talk about learning a lesson the hard way! It's bad enough if your parakeet nips you from on your shoulder – now imagine the facial damage a large bird like a macaw could do! Can you say, "Corrective Surgery"?

Oh, and the rule itself is valid for any place the bird is able to go; not just your shoulder. Any room, any piece of furniture, lighting fixture, treasured first edition book, or other living creature becomes the territory of the bird if "Dr. Fluffington" is permitted to go there without being immediately removed.

One Must "Officially" Enter the Flock by Greeting the Other Birds

I suppose it's a matter of keeping track of which bird is where and what can be expected of whom but my birds don't want to interact with me until I verbally greet them. Since English is Dorian's primary language he'll tell me "Hello" when I enter the room but if I don't return that greeting he'll often repeat it until I do. Once I say hello he'll proceed to tell me whatever's on his mind (usually apples, kiwi, or "Pet the Bird!"). Of course, the exception to this rule is when he's either really hungry or really, really REALLY wants to come out of his cage.

One Must "Officially" Exit the Flock by Saying Goodbye to the Other Birds

I think it makes birds anxious to see a flock member leave the area without indicating how long it'll be gone. Not by the clock certainly; none of my birds know or care what time it is – the position of the sun is as close to timekeeping as they get. What they're looking for is whether a valued flock member (and all members, even those they may dislike are highly valued) is going off to a puddle for a quick drink or intends to fly for several miles to find a mate and shouldn't be expected back into the flock until sundown. Because of this, one should always give to other flock members an indication of how long you'll be absent.

If Al or I are just going to go into the kitchen to make a sandwich or stepping outside to get the mail we'll say "Goodbye - I'll be right back." Every time we do this we fulfill the promise to return right away and the birds stay calm and quiet. If either of us neglects to say this Dorian will start to peep anxiously and make motions that indicate he wants to fly off his perch to find whoever has gone away. He remains anxious until the missing flock member returns. This is also true of "nap time" or going to the bathroom. Dorian needs to know where we'll be at all times.

If I'm going out of the house somewhere that will keep me from home for more than ten or fifteen minutes I'll tell the birds that I'm "going for a ride in the car", and we each say "goodbye" (usually several times). This lets them know I'll be gone for a long time and they shouldn't worry. Once I return I again join the flock by saying hello to everyone.

Nap Time is to be Respected

As you can imagine, prey animals sleep very lightly and the slightest sound can awaken them. With this in mind it will come as no surprise that birds (especially in the wild) lose a lot of sleep every night. Because of this, birds enjoy naps every day. It's probably because of this constant need to catch up on sleep that we've found our birds are always respectful whenever any of us settles down to a nap. The exception to this is when perceived danger appears in the form of, oh, a mailman, the gardener, or an obviously dangerous elderly person taking a slow stroll up the street in front of the house.

Sunrise is the Time to Wake Up (Birdy Alarm Clock)

No, it doesn't matter that you were up until 4am the previous night watching another Twilight Zone marathon – that's **your** problem. The day starts with the sun, thank-you-very-much. That's the rule. Daylight means birds are awake and they will loudly call out their presence to the world. The only way to overcome it is to cover the bird with a dark enough cover that he can't see the daylight in the morning. Now you know why we keep the blinds CLOSED in our house until after Al and I are out of bed.

In the Morning Birds Must Announce Their Presence To The World

As mentioned before, many birds call out in the morning to identify where flock members or other flock groups are situated. Dorian carries on this instinctive behavior in English, for which we're exceedingly grateful. He'll go through quite a number of his favorite phrases with some whistles and peeping thrown in for good measure.

For Polgara and Rover however, who are far less "civilized", morning reveille consists of trumpeting, calling, and giving out yells that would make Tarzan proud. These are performed either simultaneously or sequentially. Of the three birds, Polgara's voice during this daily exercise is the most piercing. Her native habitat is the Amazon jungle where it takes a lot of voice to be heard through all those trees and in competition with all those other animals making their own morning announcements. Sadly, Polgara's voice is of the EXACT pitch and frequency to seriously hurt one's ears. Al actually has distinct hearing loss that can be traced to spending too many years too close to Polgara when she shouts out.

Sunset is Time to Find a Roost the for Night

I've noticed that both Rover and Polgara, whose cage dominates the front window in our home, become nervous and fidgety when sundown begins. It doesn't help that my house faces the southwest so they get a lovely view of every sunset. The approaching darkness means diminished vision and the danger of nocturnal predators. Why, tonight might be the night that the new play gym Rover's been suspicious of decides to roll over to the cage and grab him with its silvery food dishes and gobble him up! Hey, it could happen, right? He and Polgara settle down as soon as I close the blinds and cover their cage. Sunset =

BAD. Light = GOOD. Dorian doesn't suffer at this time the way the others do but he *does* start to fluff up his feathers and settle down for some pre-bedtime cuddling.

In the Evening Birds Should Announce Their Sleeping Spot To The Neighborhood

This activity is not as mandatory as the morning shout-out; especially in our little flock. Sometimes the sight of sunset will trigger Rover and Pol to tell us all about it but sometimes they'd rather ignore the issue and concentrate on arguing over the toy they both only want because they think the other bird wants it. Dorian's never caught on to the evening announcement routine; he's usually too busy concentrating on soliciting cuddles, scratches and extra tidbits of food.

Being Covered Means Birdies MUST Settle Down for the Night (with some exceptions)

When Al and I have decided it's time for the birds to be put to bed we put Dorian in his sleeping box (Kennel Cab) and cover it with a dark blanket. We also take a large sheet of felt (72" by four yards) and cover the cage Polgara and Rover share. This covering is the signal that all noise and cavorting is to stop and they are to settle down and go to sleep. For the most part the birds respect this rule, however there are exceptions. Sometimes Rover decides he doesn't want to go to sleep yet so he'll pull the cover off the cage. Yes, 72" x 4 yards of black felt get systematically pulled, a few inches at a time, until they float gracefully to the floor, at which time he feels free to frolic and jump around to his heart's content.

We, on the other hand, usually object to this behavior (it's just like a kid who doesn't want to go to bed – "C'mon, mom, just 10 more minutes on YouTube? Please??") so we've devised a simple but effective counter-measure. Rover always tries to pull the cover off toward the side of the cage facing the window, so we use a large brooch safety pin (about four inches long) to pin the cover onto the cage on the opposite side. So far it's worked perfectly. I know he'll catch on eventually and just pull the cover off from the other side but I've got another brooch pin…

Dorian settles down quietly for the most part but since his sleeping box is next to the sofa from which Al and I converse or watch movies or TV, Dorian feels free to add comments throughout the evening until we go to bed ourselves.

"Thank you" is expressed with the Beak

Of course it is. No hands, right? And they sometimes acknowledge the giving of an object by first taking into their mouth a finger on the hand offering the object. Not every time but fairly often. This can be rather scary, as it appears that your generosity is about to be paid for with your blood. Stay calm. You reach to Dorian with a nice chunk of apple and he doesn't reach for the fruit, he reaches for your forefinger. He'll take it in his mouth and give a squeeze. Not a bite. A squeeze. Then he'll take the apple. Personally I often find this annoying and sometimes I move my hand out of his mouth. Does that make me ungrateful, or at the least, impolite? Well, maybe…

*To Greet A New Bird, It's Polite To Allow It To Touch Your Tongue***

Birds' tongues are very different than ours. They're dry and blunt and are used more to process food than taste it. In fact, birds have far less of a sense of taste in their tongues than we do but a lot more sensory receptors. This is why birds explore their surroundings by touching everything with their tongues. Birds that are not acquainted with each other will sometimes touch each other's tongues to learn about each other – somewhat along the lines of a dog sniffing another dog.

Please keep in mind that, just as you are not encouraged to sniff a dog you're just meeting, you are also not encouraged to present your tongue to a bird you're just meeting. If the bird shows an interest in exploring you in this fashion we highly recommend you offer a fingertip instead – and if you're very interested in making a friend of this bird, touch your tongue with your fingertip before you offer the fingertip to the bird. There will be enough saliva on it for the bird to figure you out.

Always remember that this greeting is NOT REQUIRED.

** HEY, YOU'RE A HUMAN! DO NOT ATTEMPT THIS GREETING UNLESS YOU ARE VERY WELL ACQUAINTED WITH THE BIRD, OR YOU ACTUALLY *ARE* ANOTHER BIRD. You COULD get bitten!

INSTINCTIVE FEARS

All animals have instinctive fears of one sort or another and certainly prey animals like birds do. You might think that a bird who lives safely in a roomy cage in a loving home would have nothing to be afraid of but you'd be mistaken. Some fears are ingrained and inherited, and most make sense though some have me stumped.

The first instinctive fear has already been mentioned. Anything unfamiliar is taken as threatening and must be approached with extreme caution.

Anything appearing over a bird's head is taken as a potential predator, as is anything with predator's eyes – both facing forward the way ours do, or like a dog or cat or owl.

Sudden noises, movements, or appearances are so threatening to birds that their autonomic nervous systems immediately throw them into panic mode whenever this happens, even if the person who appeared without warning is their beloved human. They can't help it.

It should be noted that some species of birds have individualized fears. An interesting article in "Nature: The International Weekly Journal of Science" entitled "Birds Born to Fear Red" (July 31, 2009 by Matt Kaplan) states that the bold color red is intimidating to certain finches. (read the article online here:

http://www.nature.com/news/2009/090731/full/news.2009.760.html)

It makes us wonder if the bright, red tail of the African Grey Parrot is used to intimidate other species. Since they're generally not terribly aggressive, does their tail "warn off" other birds competing for food or territory? Or perhaps is it a signal so they can find one another in their natural habitat?

Well, to get back to the subject of instinctive fears, here are a few we've noticed in our flock.

This one makes sense: A fear that's shared by all three of our  birds is baseball caps. Anyone coming into the house wearing a baseball cap elicits all sorts of fear responses from all three birds. They fluff out their feathers to look as large as they can, sometimes opening their wings. Rover might trumpet and Dorian makes a rumbling growling sound.

Why? What's a harmless baseball cap ever done to our birds? Maybe they support the wrong team? The color turns them off?

No. Think about it for just a second and you'll come up with the answer. To a bird, the brim of a baseball cap looks alarmingly like the bill of a predatory bird, and since most people wearing them are pretty tall as measured off the ground, they appear to be predatory birds on the hunt. Once the offender removes the hat the birds calm down, though they might remain suspicious for a while.

Here's one we're unsure about. Though Dorian has always been transported from his cage to his T-stand or playpen on a ¾"x 4' dowel, he is very afraid of long sticks, such as broom or mop handles. He reacts to these even more urgently than he does to baseball caps, actually screaming in  alarm when one comes near him. Apparently this is not an uncommon fear among parrots but we've been unable to find any credible explanation for it. The only thing we can think of is that these handles might remind him of snakes? Now, he's never actually seen a snake, or even a toy rubber one, and snakes are nearly never stretched out full length, which might make them look like a broom handle but it's the only reason we can think of for his fear. (He's never seen a predatory bird either, for that matter). At the same time, neither of the other birds appear to be put off by broom handles or other similar, stick-like objects. If you have a good explanation, please let us know.

Now, this last one baffles me entirely. I have a pair of black and white striped socks that sets Dorian off something fierce. All he needs to do is see them and he goes into attack stance and growls and will actually leap at them (whether my feet are in them or not). I have no idea why he reacts this way to these innocent socks. Was his grandfather stepped on by a zebra?? I'll probably never know.

DOES HE TALK? THE QUESTION IS, DOES HE EVER SHUT UP?!

African Greys are famous for their ability to imitate sounds and speech and of course we were very eager for Dorian to intelligibly communicate with us. We started with whistles, which we figured would come pretty naturally to any bird, and he quickly picked up simple whistles and reacted happily when we praised and petted him for imitating us. Many recommend against this practice, as it encourages whistling instead of using words. We didn't know this at the time, actually but luckily it never seemed to impede his eagerness to speak English.

His precocious ability to imitate sounds was displayed at an early stage when I was napping one day and suddenly heard Dorian making an odd, growling sort of sound. Alarmed, I rushed to Al and described what I hoped was not an indication of some horrible, fatal malady in our little bappy, and was surprised and somewhat put out when Al started to laugh; explaining that the bird was merely imitating my SNORING as I slept! (I have since obtained a CPAP mask, thank you very much – I have sleep apnea. I officially no longer snore. So THERE.)

It's interesting that Dorian CHOOSES what words he wants to say. He readily picked up the meaning of "Dinner" and uses it appropriately however he's never caught on to "Breakfast" or "Lunch". Perhaps he's too hungry at that time to pay attention to polite conversation, or perhaps it's simply a matter of his not being aware of the concept of time. This is demonstrated also by his intermittent use of "good night" instead of "good morning" when we start our day.

Sometimes if he hears a sound or word he REALLY likes Dorian can accurately pick it up almost instantly. One day Al was in a playful mood and when I asked what he wanted for breakfast he said, "Coffee-coffee-coffee!" Dorian instantly picked up the phrase, and though he's never tasted it (caffeine, you know) he still likes the sound of the phrase and we'll sometimes hear him say "coffee-coffee-coffee!" throughout the day.

Sometimes he invents words. This is apparently not all that unusual for these birds. For example, Dorian loves chocolate and he also loves gummy bears. One day long ago we brought home some fudge and offered him a small morsel of it. He LOVED it! Spontaneously he said "want more chocolate gummy!" We were surprised and rather proud of him – fudge tastes like chocolate but FEELS like a gummy bear! To this day he'll specify 'chocolate gummy' if he wants some fudge (but don't think for a moment that he gets some every time he asks).

He did the same thing with walnuts, though he was more accurate that time. When we introduced him to a chocolate-covered walnut he independently identified it as "choc-walnut". I may be prejudiced in his favor but I can't help thinking he's TERRIBLY clever!

Non-verbal sounds, such as car alarms, telephones ringing, and various whistles all come to him quite quickly and without apparent effort. Others take time and a great deal of study and practice.

When a word interests him, Dorian will spend a great deal of effort to learn it. A good example of this is the way he learned the word "kiwi". From the first moment he tasted a piece of dried kiwi, he adored it and was determined to learn the word so he could ask for it accurately (and frequently).

As we usually do, when we handed him the fruit we used the word. "Here's some kiwi, Dorian," we'd say. "This is called 'kiwi'". A day or two after being introduced to the food, he started saying "Wiwi. Want Wiwi." Just like correcting a child, we would repeat the correct pronunciation and I even pointed out that the word begins with the same sound as the word 'kiss', which he already knew. 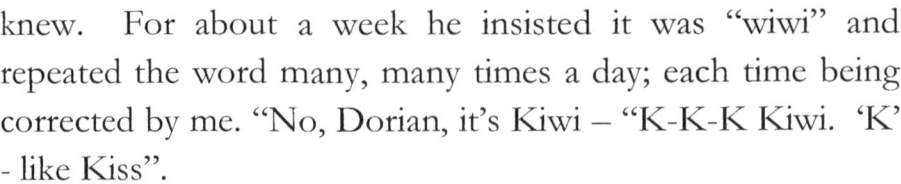 For about a week he insisted it was "wiwi" and repeated the word many, many times a day; each time being corrected by me. "No, Dorian, it's Kiwi – "K-K-K Kiwi. 'K' - like Kiss".

Abruptly one morning he got the word right and received not only great praise and petting but he also got a slice of dried kiwi for his trouble. After this he spent another week endlessly repeating "kiwi" until he was sure he'd gotten the word down and would never forget it. This is pretty much the way he learns all his words. He practices endlessly until he's got it, then it subsides into just another part of his extensive vocabulary (lists of his commonly used words and phrases are included toward the end of this book).

The very first time we realized Dorian was able to make up his own sentences came when he was not quite one year old. Al and our daughter Rachael were snacking on pieces of a lovely, ripe watermelon and sharing bits of it with the birds. Dorie really enjoyed the fruit and gobbled down every piece he was given. After a short while Al decided the bird had had enough and stopped giving him any. Dorian responded by spontaneously saying "Want More!" - a phrase we had NOT taught him.

Since that time Dorie's been stringing words together to let us know what he wants and often he'll come out with a new sentence seemingly out of left field. Just the other day he surprised us with a new one: One of my favorite snacks is Pepperidge Farm's Captiva cookies; a large, soft chocolate cookie with soft chocolate chips in it. I have a feeling that this is what Dorian meant when he spontaneously came out with "Want gummy the chocolate cookie." Tastes like a chocolate cookie but feels like a gummy? Another point for the parrot!

Dorian speaks English for much of the day; especially when he's alone. He'll quietly babble to himself just like a small child will do when playing by himself. He'll go through many of his favorite phrases and songs, asking questions and providing the answers, and sometimes telling himself jokes.

Oh, haven't I mentioned that Dorian knows what a joke is? We discovered this amazing fact many years ago when he told one to us. Here's how it happened: One of the games we play involves animal sounds. "What does a dog say?" we'll ask, and he'll appropriately answer with his imitation of a dog's woof. "What does a cow say" results in a prolonged, basso-profundo "moooooo". Dorian also knows what cats and owls say, and sometimes says, "are you a good owl?" (he also does a decent imitation of Maurice Chevalier's nasal but charming "honh-honh-honh"). Sometimes we ask the questions and sometimes Dorian asks.

We were playing this game one day when Dorian said, "What does a dog say – meow! – HA-HA-HA!" Yes. He asked for a dog sound, made the cat sound, and then laughed at his own joke! He still plays that joke on us, once every long while.

Since Dorie used to stay in Al's office all day long he often heard Al on the phone and picked up what a phone conversation is like. Sometimes when we get a telephone call Dorian will helpfully have an entire conversation for us, saying "Hello, uh-huh, hold on, okay, goodbye."

Though I'm told that some birds (especially mynahs) can accurately imitate the actual voice of their human, to my ears Dorian doesn't do this. He does, however, have several tones of voice in which he speaks. When addressing Al he'll speak in a lower voice than he'll use when addressing me. This of course may be in imitation of Al's much lower voice however I can always tell which is Dorian and which is Al. It's actually kind of cute when he speaks in "sotto voce"; a very low basso profundo voice and says his name this way.

Dorian is also able to whisper. "Can You Whisper" is a phrase I taught him years ago and while he is able to whisper his words he apparently doesn't like doing it and only occasionally whispers back to me. I wonder if it's because he's aware that it's harder to hear? Not sure about that one...

His pronunciation of words can sometimes be baffling. For years he would say "Birdie Beh-TIE". Not knowing what he was trying to get across, we weren't able to correct him and the phrase remained a mystery until we finally figured out that he was saying "Birdie Bedtime" but putting the accent on the wrong syllable. Once we made this realization, correcting him was a snap. This was why we stopped letting him watch Sesame Street by himself – there were too many unintelligibile phrases we couldn't figure out.

An interesting thing I've noticed is that while I call Dorian "Bappy" all day long, and of course he's excellent at learning and appropriately using words, he's never once spoken the word "bappy." He understands that this is a word I use with him and the other two birds but he's never even attempted to say it. This makes me wonder what he thinks I mean by the word. He does call me "Ducky" and "Dru" (though he's never said "Al". I suspect he thinks we're both to be called "Dru") but in his mind "bappy" is something only I say, and only in reference to him and the other birds.

This brings me to another mystery – sometimes I'm not entirely sure what he means when he says certain things in context. Sometimes, if Dorian asks for something specific and I give it to him he'll say "Dorie good bird." Does he mean HE is a good bird or does me mean I'M a good bird? I'm never quite sure.

While much of his thoughts center on himself, I know he's making a statement specifically about me when I leave the house. I tell him to "be a good bird" and in return he tells me to "be a good boo." He never uses the word "boo" in any other context. Is my confusion caused by his lack of knowledge of pronouns or his different world view? I haven't figured it out yet.

Oh, by the way, you should always keep in mind that birds' ability to instantly pick up sounds, words and phrases includes vulgarity and any incriminating remarks you might utter that catches the bird's fancy. If you've been using the word, don't be at all surprised if, after telling the bird he cannot have a treat, he replies with "SHIT!" or "DAMMIT!" Yes, he has a good sense of how these words are used.

In the same vein, be sure you don't keep repeating in front of the bird how much you dislike your boss, neighbor, mother-in-law or anyone else who might some day visit your home. You never know when that bird is going to decide to say, "Dammit, I hate that stupid boss of mine!" A word to the wise…

How Parrots Actually Accomplish Pronouncing Words

Parrots obviously lack lips with which to form words, and in fact they don't even have vocal cords, so you may wonder how they actually go about pronouncing "Wanna come out" so effectively.

Without getting technical, a bird's throat contains structures that allow it to manipulate the air flow and shape of their larynx, which produces the wide variety of sounds they make, from speech to the phone ringing to the sound of your car alarm going off. The bottom line is that their speech originates entirely from within their throats. Thought you'd like to know.

THE TRANSFORMATION OF WORDS

Sometimes the words Dorie uses change meaning. For example, while we were crossing the country, Dorian, who was somewhat traumatized by the trip, began to ask for "gummy" a great deal however when we offered him a gummy bear it was clearly not what he wanted. He's never been able to learn concept words like "attention" or "comfort" which is what he really wanted, so he transformed the word "gummy" to have this meaning. Now, when he REALLY wants a gummy he'll ask for "gummy bear". I guess he's given a new meaning to the term "comfort food."

There's a game Rachael plays with the bird that involves singing the theme song from the old Adam West "Batman" TV series. At first, Dorie would sing "Batman! Do-Do-Do-Do-Do-Do-Do-Do-Batman!" Well, that quickly changed from "Batman" to "Bat-bird" and now seems interchangeable when singing the theme song between "Bat-bird" and "Duck-bird". I guess it depends on whether he's feeling just ducky or a little batty. Sorry about the pun; I couldn't help myself…

Sometimes the bird will experiment with changing the pronunciation of a word to see if he likes it better, or to see how we respond to it. He did this with the name of our Amazon parrot, changing 'Polgara' to 'Polgaro". Speculation might suggest that he did this because we call our cockatoo both 'Rover' and 'Rovie', and of course, quite often we call Dorian 'Dorie'. Did he think Polgara needed a nickname? Your guess is as good as mine.

When raising either a human child or a bird, consistency is very important. This lesson was brought home to me by the inadvertent transformation of the word "Goodbye." Dorian already knew that "Goodbye" is the word we use when we're leaving the house. Well, I mistakenly said "goodbye" when I was going into Al's and my shared office; a room out of Dorian's sight but still within the house. Being that I was not actually leaving the house (i.e. the flock's tree?) I should not have used that word because almost immediately he began to use "Hello" and "Goodbye" interchangeably whenever I left the house or came back into it. I had confused him about the proper word usage. It took a while of being more consistent to correct his understanding.

Some words get changed seemingly because he's just plain decided to change them. One of his favorite treats is M&Ms and he asks for them by name, though sometimes he'll ask for "M & Dorian" or "M & Apple". I suppose the latter is requested when he's not quite sure what he wants. "M & Dorian" might have grown out of "M&M for Dorian" but I can't be certain.

YES, THEY'RE THINKING AND REASONING. MY FAVORITE EXAMPLES

A study reported in early August, 2012 by the journal "Proceedings of the Royal Society B – Biological Sciences" showed that African Grey Parrots can logically solve a problem that three year old humans had difficulty figuring out. Read one of the reports about the study here: http://www.dailymail.co.uk/sciencetech/article-2185209/How-parrots-smarter-children-monkeys-dogs.html in this article published in the Daily Mail Online.

Another article, this one published online at Care2.com entitled *"Scientists Declare: Animals Are as Aware as Humans"* mentions, among other things, that African Grey parrots show "near human-like levels of consciousness". Read this fascinating article here:

http://www.care2.com/greenliving/scientists-declare-animals-are-as-aware-as-humans.html

We've seen over and over the clear evidence that our birds use reason and logic to solve the many problems of parrot life such as how to get fed, how to reach those delicious-looking vertical blinds hanging by the front window, or how to get some much-needed attention.

Dorie went nuts for cheesecake!

One day Dorian was standing on the T-stand in our family room as usual when I walked past him with a slice of cheesecake on a plate. He leaned toward me and said, "Go in your bowl." Well, this is what we always say to him when we feed him, and not thinking about it, I replied to him, saying, "Yes, Dorie, there's food in your bowl. Go in your bowl."

This wasn't the desired response so he repeated "Go in your bowl," to which I replied in the same way again.

This frustrated him, and this time his inflection was very insistent: "GO IN YOUR BOWL!" Hearing the change in his voice, I turned back to him, cheesecake still in hand and said, "what do you want, Dorian?"

I could nearly see the little cogs and wheels turning in his head as he clearly put his mind to the problem and thought out a solution. I was not getting the message and it was important to him to figure out a way to communicate what he had in mind. In a minute he came out with the following sentence: "WANT GO IN YOUR BOWL". I was quite startled because we had never said that to him – he figured it out and created the sentence all by himself.

Now the cogs and wheels started turning in MY head until I figured out that HE wanted to go in MY bowl – he simply didn't have command of the proper pronouns.

"Is this what you want?" I asked as I held out the cheesecake to him. His answer was to nearly dive-bomb the plate as he gobbled an enormous chunk of cheesecake. Quite impressed with his reasoning, I shared the cheesecake with him, and he's loved it ever since.

On another day Al and I were extremely busy and couldn't let Dorian out of his cage. His response was to repeatedly make a shrill, ear-splitting peeping sound he hoped would get him some kind of attention, even if it was negative attention. Under other circumstances we might have shouted out to him such phrases as "Dorian, stop that!" or "Dorian, what are you doing? Stop Peeping!!" On this occasion we were too involved in whatever-it-was and just ignored his attempts. Finally, apparently frustrated at his lack of success, Dorie filled in for us by shouting out, "What Are You Doing? I'm Peeping!"

Like all flock animals, our little birdie-boy constantly wants the comfort and pleasure of our attention. One day he came out with something that so impressed us that Al wrote down the date it happened. On November 1, 2010 Al and I were quite busy doing something that kept us from giving Dorian the proper amount of adoration, petting and food treats he feels are his due. After repeated attempts to get our attention failed, Dorian finally succeeded by coming out with, "What are you doing? Come over here and tickle the bird!" Well, what would you have done? Yeah, we went over there and tickled him!

It's lovely that he's able to tell us precisely what he wants in so decisive a manner. When he was young and lived in Al's office it was not unusual for Al to stay up quite late into the night in front of his computer (he's a computer geek with more certifications after his name than anyone I've ever known). One evening as it grew later and later Dorian looked over the monitor at Al and said, "good night." Focusing on the problem he was working on, Al absently bid the bird good night and continued what he was doing. Once more Dorian told him, "Good night." Once more he was ignored. At last, frustrated and really wanting to go to sleep Dorian shouted out sternly, "Bad Bird! Good Night!" Al finally got the message, shut down the computer (and the light switch) and let the bird get some rest.

Ready to go to bedtime

Another of my favorite examples of the way the bird thinks is this one that we mentioned earlier: Whenever I leave the house I not only say goodbye, I usually say "You be a good bird" or "You be a good boy." Dorian also hears us call Polgara, our only female bird, a "good girl." He uses this noun accurately and never refers to Rover as a girl, but he never refers to me as a girl either. Perhaps he's not entirely sure what Al and I are, though he clearly understands that we're not birds. Since we've never identified ourselves as humans or people or persons per se he's made up his own designation for me, and when I tell him to "be a good bird", he's very likely to tell me "you be a good boo." He came up with that word by himself. I'm still not sure what he thinks it means but he only uses it with me.

In another vein, Rover the Cockatoo doesn't speak English but he's wonderfully intelligent as well and what interests him is different than what interests Dorian. He's the great escape artist of the family. We hadn't lived with him for very long before we discovered that opening the doors to his cage was as easy for him as waking up in the morning. We quickly put combination locks on all the cage doors and he carefully observed us whenever we opened one of them. It wasn't long before Rover began flipping the combination lock up to face him and using his beak to turn the little black dial with the numbers on it. We're just grateful that he never learned to count or he would have figured out the locks in no time.

Sometimes Rover's great intelligence outwits our best attempts to keep his enthusiasm and curiosity under control. The cage he shares with Polgara is just inside our large front window which is covered by vertical blinds. Now, we're certainly aware of the great delight he takes in chewing on vertical blinds, since he did so in our home in California. With this in mind, when we moved into our new house we carefully placed the cage a good distance from the vertical blinds. Not to be defeated however, it wasn't long before Rover was able to stretch out his foot and leg through the bars of the cage to grab one of those verticals, which he happily chewed holes into before we caught him. Frustrated, we moved the cage even further from the window, measuring the length of Rover's leg plus his extended claws to be sure we were moving the cage far enough away that he couldn't possibly reach those verticals. Stupid humans! Was Rover to be defeated? Not on your fluffy powder down feathers, he wasn't! Not long after moving the cage we returned from doing errands to find that not only had he chewed on another vertical, he had gnawed one in half!! How the devil did he accomplish this?!? We discovered the secret not long after moving the cage even further away. You see, he made another attempt on the fascinating and doubtless delicious vertical blinds and this time we saw him doing it. This wonderful and too-smart-for-our-own-good bird went over to the corner of the cage nearest the verticals, held onto the bars with one foot and his beak, reached through the bars with the other foot, and vigorously flapped his wings, causing the verticals to billow toward him in this Rover-caused wind! Luckily for us we had moved the cage far enough away that he was (finally!) unable to catch them. We're still amazed at his ingenuity and problem-solving ability!

BIRDS' MOST IMPORTANT LANGUAGE – BODY LANGUAGE

If one is going to attempt to live with birds one absolutely must learn what they're saying with their body language. You know what that is – we see it in other humans all the time. What the mouth says may not match what the body is telling you. "I'm glad to meet you" coupled with arms folded defensively across the chest shows a clearly mixed message. Since body language is mostly unconscious in humans it would be a wise choice to take the words with a grain of salt and believe what the body is saying.

The one item of bird body language that's most important for a human to recognize is what birds do when they're about to relieve themselves. They sort of squat down a bit and wiggle their tail.

Dorian in "potty posture". Look out below!

If they're on a perch they'll lean forward a bit and lift their tail as they let go their droppings. If they're standing on a table or other flat surface they'll take a bit of a step forward just before letting go. Seeing this preparatory behavior gives you maybe one or two seconds of warning so you can remove the bird from your best trousers or Aunt Sarah's handmade tablecloth and put him on a more appropriate place before it's too late.

Eye pinning: You'll be talking to Dorian and suddenly the pupils of his eyes will become tiny. This is called eye pinning (as though his pupils become pinpoints – get it?). Greys and many other parrot species do this deliberately and there are two basic reasons for it. The first, and more "friendly" reason is that they're concentrating or being interested in what's going on. The second one is when they're angry or upset, and you'd better keep your fingers at a safe distance. You can tell the difference by paying attention to the rest of his body. If his feathers are smoothed down and he looks relaxed, it's the former but if his feathers are fluffed out and he's leaning forward as though ready to jump off his perch, watch out!

Quivering: If his entire body is quivering it probably means he's frightened. Try to figure out where he's looking, as this may reveal the source of his anxiety. If only his chest is quivering it's believed he's showing contentment and positive emotion. The epitome of the "happy bappy!"

Scratch Like A Chicken: In the wild, Greys, like so many other birds, scratch at the ground to loosen the soil so they can get at something or dig their way somewhere. Dorian will do this too, apparently to overcome an obstacle, such as a door barring his way into the bathroom. It almost appears as though he thinks he can dig his way under the door. Good luck with that, Dorie...

Bowing his head near your hand: When Dorian wants to be petted or scratched or wants help with some uncomfortable new feather quills around his neck he'll bow his head down and rest his beak on your leg or any other convenient leaning post, inviting you to give him some attention and adoration. Be careful though – when in a playful mood he will often use this as a ploy to bring your fingers within biting range! This is mostly a "gotcha" sort of thing for him but if he REALLY means to hurt you he'll actually say "OW!" as he catches your finger!

Feather Fluffing: This has various meanings and has to be taken in context. Sometimes fluffing is simply a re-arrangement of feathers to shake out the dust. Sometimes it's because he's relaxed and is settling down to nap.

An angry, aggressive Dorian

Keep an eye on his entire body though; if he's angry or feels threatened he'll fluff out his feathers to look as large as possible, and he'll lean forward as though ready to leap.

Aggressive postures: These include leaning forward with feathers fluffed, fanning the tail, swaying from side to side, and sometimes making noises. Dorian will make a growling sound if he feels threatened while Rover will go into a full wing and crest display and will either hiss or trumpet at the (painful to hear) top of his lungs.

Contented postures: Standing on the perch with feathers just slightly puffed out is usually a sign of contentment; possibly an overture to a nap. This is especially true if the bird raises one foot up with the toes curled. If you've ever wondered how birds stay on their perches while asleep it's because when their toes relax they naturally go into a curled position, making holding onto their perch much easier.

Relaxing bappy

Full eye looking: The main way you can tell whether an animal is a predator or a prey animal is by looking at the placement of their eyes. We predators have forward-facing eyes that allow us binocular vision and wonderful depth perception so we know exactly when to reach out and grab that impala or fish or chicken (or hamburger) we want to dine on. Prey animals need to see us predators from every angle so they have eyes on the sides of their head, giving them 360 degrees of vision. Because of this, birds don't have to look directly at you to see you however if they are VERY interested in something (including you) they will turn their heads so one eye is pointed directly at the object of interest.

Interestingly enough, birds tend to favor one eye over the other when studying an object (like your slice of pizza) and many parrots and cockatoos have a strong tendency to be not only left-eyed but left footed as well. I've read some articles that explain that these tendencies are related to brain dominance, just as they are in humans. One article claimed that 100% of the sulphur-crested cockatoos they tested were left-footed. Rover, our Umbrella cockatoo is also left-footed however, both our parrots must be ambidextrous (probably just to stand out from the crowd) because I've seen them pick things up with either foot. Actually, Dorian prefers to get up onto our left hands, possibly because he prefers to step up with his right foot but as I type this he's eating something while holding it in his left foot. It figures that two out of three of our birds do things differently from other parrots!

Parrots do a lot of things that we humans do, and they do them in the same way. They stretch, yawn, cough, scratch itches, sneeze, and pick their noses when the need arises, though of course they do so with their talons. Happily, I've never heard of a person picking their nose with their toes, though I imagine it's not entirely beyond the realm of possibility. Frankly I could live the rest of my life quite contentedly without ever visualizing such a thing; how about you?

Switching for a moment to Rover the cockatoo, his crest (the feathers on his head) is a wonderful barometer of what's on his mind. If it's down and relaxed, so is the bird. If it's raised up somewhat it indicates alertness and interest. If Rover's crest is held entirely erect it means he's worried, and if his crest is all the way up 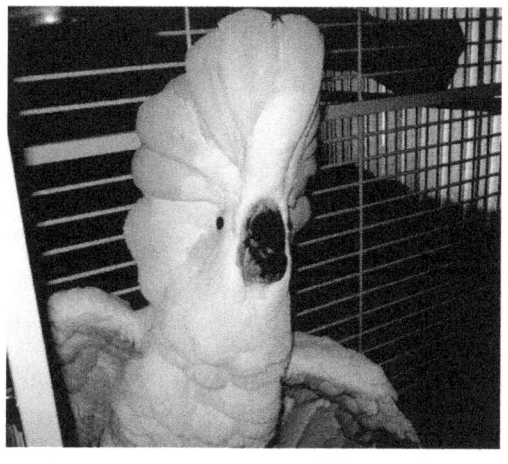 and he stretches out his wings he's seriously alarmed! I suppose you could liken this to a human's hair on the back of the neck, which is said to stand straighter the more nervous and alert one becomes.

In the photo above Rover is in a nearly full display – his crest is all the way up and his wings are about halfway spread. He did this in reaction to my camera, which he has taken as threatening; especially since I brought it inside his cage. If he was completely upset his wings would have been completely spread and he would have trumpeted loudly. He had actually gotten to the point of clacking his beak in a warning manner. Yes, as soon as I took the photo I backed out of the cage and he almost immediately settled down again.

Birds also do some things we don't do, which of course makes it harder for us to interpret. Dorian often bobs his head up and down at seemingly random times. If we bob our heads back at him sometimes he'll continue this behavior and sometimes he won't. Experts' explanations for head-bobbing vary but the consensus seems to be that it's just plain communication. Maybe it's an expression of affection - I've asked Dorian but he's never specified.

Something else he does is droop his wings. Sometimes he puts his wings slightly out and lets them droop downward. I'm not sure what he means by this – I've read that it might be related to courting behavior and I've also read that it might indicate the bird isn't feeling well. It isn't the same as when he opens his wings slightly as though eager to jump off the perch. Go ask the bird what he means but make sure you don't hold your breath while waiting for an answer. I prefer to think it means he's so relaxed and happy he's "letting down his hair" as it were. In truth, I simply don't know what he means.

TERRITORIAL & MANIPULATIVE BEHAVIOR

Naturally curious, birds want to go everywhere, see everything, and chew on or eat everything. Dorian is no exception but there ARE areas of the house we just plain don't want him in. This requires a lot of effort, as once we take him out of his cage he gets bored and jumps down to go exploring. This is in compliance with the "Bird Rule" that once we've permitted him access to any area it now belongs to him and he's free to go there any time he likes and do anything that occurs to him. Take Heed! He will assume that an admonition NOT to climb onto the office chair means "just for that moment" and as soon as he's been removed he'll attempt to go there again. We repeatedly remove him onto his carrying stick with a firm "NO!" however he's never caught on that we mean it as a permanent injunction. No doubt this is due to birds' lack of a concept of time but for nearly 19 years this behavior has remained consistent.

When Dorie wants to come out of his cage he'll say, "want to come out," but he also uses this phrase after he's out of the cage when he wants to come down off the play gym and go exploring. What he really means is, "I want to be unrestrained."

Like all little children, Dorian often tries to get what he wants by manipulation, though also like any kid, his methods are not what you'd call sophisticated. For example, he knows that when he's hungry I give him attention by feeding him and talking to him so sometimes when he wants my attention he'll say, "Want Apple." Having just fed him, I'll reply, "There's apple in your bowl, Dorian. Go in your bowl." Tricky ol' Dorian will pick up the pieces of apple in his bowl and drop them to the floor of his cage where they fall beneath the grating where he can't reach them, then once more call out, "Want Apple." This ploy has never once worked but he keeps trying it over and over and over. Can't fault him for a lack of tenacity.

When we say living with birds takes patience, we really mean it.

TRAUMATIC BEHAVIOR

This is so important for you to know! As we've said before, birds don't like their lives, environment, or flock to change. In fact, they take major changes worse than we humans do. Changes of any kind need to be made slowly and the more consistent the rest of their lives remain, the easier they'll adapt. It took Dorie about two days to accept being put onto the new bird playpen and another few days to become comfortable enough to explore and play on it. Polgara and Rover wouldn't do more than look at it for nearly a week before we were able to put Pol on it without her leaping off to fly back to her cage. It took Rover another three tries before he'd stay on it.

The same is true with their food. New foods have to be introduced gradually or they will simply be rejected.

Birds have emotions and react to various situations just as we do. It's not very unusual for a bird whose environment has changed drastically to start displaying traumatic behaviors, like screaming, chewing on or plucking out their feathers, or self-mutilation in which they chew on their own flesh.

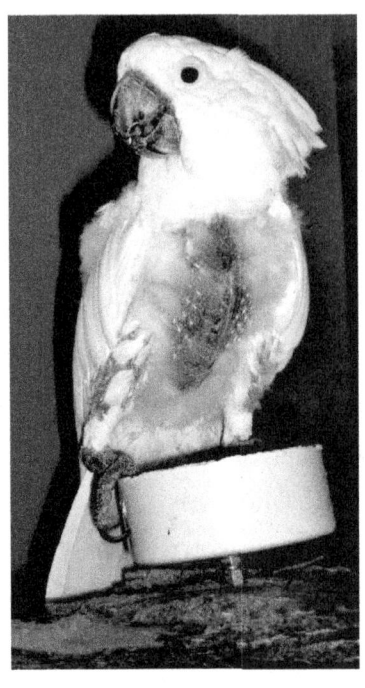 

Babe, an Umbrella Cockatoo who has been picking out the feathers on his chest.

Photo courtesy of Florida Parrot Rescue

Maui, a Blue & Gold Macaw, also feather-picking.

Photo courtesy of Florida Parrot Rescue

These heartbreaking photos provide a small example of how emotionally birds can react. Each of their situations were slightly different but the bottom line was that the humans to whom they gave their hearts disappeared from their lives for one reason or another and they displayed their despair destructively on their own bodies. We humans must keep in mind that living with a bird is not a short-term thing; you can't suddenly decide it's too much work and abandon or give away a companion bird. The emotional damage can be devastating. Living with a companion psitticine is a life-long commitment, as their life spans are as long as ours. Please take heed.

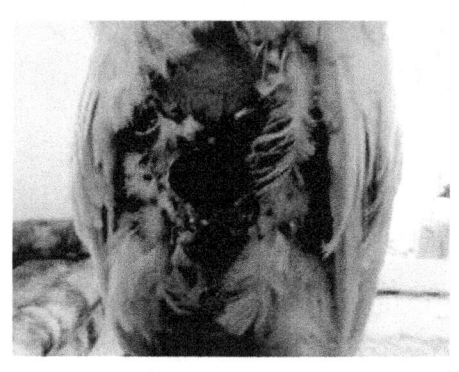

Destiny, a cockatoo who picked at her own flesh, causing this awful mutilation.

Photo courtesy of Florida Parrot Rescue

On a happier note, I'm delighted to report that the three birds shown above have all been adopted into new homes and are recovering nicely.

Long ago we knew a large Amazon parrot who was kept alone in a cage all by herself and never let out. Of her two human owners, she disliked one and though hungry for the attention of the other, never got a lot of it, and was only spoken to and not handled or offered toys. It's not surprising that this bird-without-a-flock began nervously pulling out her own feathers out of boredom, loneliness and probably some amount of despair. When counseled, the owners got a larger cage which they put in their living room (the room in which they spent most of their time), put toys in the cage, and were taught to overcome their fear of getting bitten. The bird never did "take a shine" to the owner it didn't formerly like but her relationship with the preferred owner improved as she was given much more attention and spent more "flock time". She was no longer a pariah, and though she wasn't suddenly placed in the lap of luxury and affection, her situation was improved enough to where she stopped pulling out her feathers.

What Was That Noise?

One must always keep in mind that birds are prey animals, to which caution comes naturally. In fact, it comes more than naturally, it comes autonomically! As we mentioned earlier, the sudden appearance of a moving object (human, dog, shoe flying through the air) or a sudden, unexpected sound (car horn, sudden scream, piano falling off a roof) results in an autonomic panic response. Therefore, even if you've raised "Bippy" from an egg, if you appear suddenly and shout "I LOVE YOU!" don't be surprised if he chomps down on your hand when you reach into his cage to give him a hug. He's in a panic state. He has no idea what he's doing, except surviving.

ENDEARING BEHAVIOR

We put up with birds' noise, mess, and constant demands because a lot of what they do is very endearing. This varies from specie to specie, since each has their own basic temperament . Some species want more physical attention than others, some sing more than others, some want to play with their humans more than others. In all cases, just as you're about to call your local parrot rescue organization because your "Jardine the Ripper" is driving you absolutely nuts, she'll suddenly turn around and do something that will melt your heart. Your eyes fill with little valentines as your hand unconsciously hangs up the phone and once again, you're in love.

Of course Dorian has his collection of sure-fire behaviors guaranteed to elicit forgiveness for that unexpected bite or leaving an enormous poop on the freshly-vacuumed carpet. If he knows he's made us angry (and believe me; he KNOWS) he'll suddenly start to speak in a tiny, high-pitched voice or make little baby-bird cheeps as though to say, "I'm just a cute, innocent little bappy who didn't know better." Yeah, it gets me nearly every time.

One thing he does that gets me right in the heart-strings is how he sometimes gives me a kiss. He doesn't do this every time but I get a charge out of it whenever he decides to do it.

I'll get near him and ask for a kiss, puckering up and leaning over to within an inch or two of his beak. Sometimes he'll just lean forward and touch his beak to my mouth but once in a while, instead of making a kiss sound he'll make a kind of popping sound and throw his beak forward to bonk it against my lips. In reading over this description it doesn't sound like much but his tossing his head forward to literally give me a smack in the mouth is both amusing and endearing. Okay, so he's got me in the palm of his…foot.

He frequently offers verbal kisses, making the kissy sound and saying "got a kiss for me?" but once in a while he'll say "Big Kiss!" and make a really loud, prolonged kiss sound. The Don Juan of the parrot world.

Dorian started pulling endearing or amusing tricks when he was very young. As mentioned earlier, when he was a bappy we would take him with us to many places; one of which was our local ice cream shop. We've already mentioned how much he enjoys ice cream and we used to get him a little kid's cup of his own. I'm sure it didn't hurt the shop owner's business that people would flock around the table to watch the parrot take eager bites out of the cup as well as the ice cream. Sometimes we would take one of those tiny sampling spoons and feed him the ice cream with it and on one occasion, when we weren't paying enough attention to getting the ice cream into the birdie, Dorian took that tiny spoon, held it in one foot, and fed himself! Oh, how I wish I'd had a camera! The "ooh"s and "aww"s of the spectators were nearly deafening however he only did that the one time, having quickly realized he could get more ice cream into his mouth by just jamming his beak into it.

If you'd like to see something funny enough to laugh aloud at, watch Dorie eating a gummy bear. He has a studied method to this process. First he mouths the gummy all over to soften it a bit, then he sticks it onto the point of his upper beak (maxillary rostrum, remember?) and maneuvers it with his tongue to flip it downward so he can scrape off a little biteful with his lower beak (mandibular rostrum, in case you wondered). He continues in this manner, with most of the gummy stuck to his upper beak, being flipped up and down as he munches on it, never wasting a drop.

We find it very endearing when Dorian chats throughout the evening from within his sleeping box, laughing with us whenever we laugh, and replying (mostly unintelligibly) to comments we make.

Dorian quickly learned to recognize various sounds made by a soda can. He also learned that when one drinks soda from the can a certain result is bound to occur. Long ago he learned to make burping sounds and he associates this so strongly with soda that when he simply sees a soda can he'll make a burping sound, and he's become so sharp at recognizing everything about soda cans that the other day Al simply placed a can of soda on the table and from within his sleeping box Dorian made his burping sound. He apparently enjoys making this sound; possibly from the laughter it always elicits from various visitors and friends, and since I don't drink soda he also associates soda specifically with Al;

so much so that sometimes when Al puts out the lights to go to bed and says, "Goodnight, Dorian" the bird will reply by burping for him.

THEY'RE TIDY ON THEIR OWN TERMS

Though they throw food throughout the wild world, birds are actually very clean animals, albeit on their own terms. They follow the bird rules (which you need to remember) and don't take into consideration the fact that you've just replaced the carpeting.

For example, Dorian will not relieve himself in his sleeping box. He holds it in until I take him out every morning, and if I don't hurry to put him on the playpen he will happily produce this enormous "morning sploot" on the floor, on the table, on the bed, or wherever he happens to be that is NOT his sleeping box.

Dorian relieves himself every fifteen minutes or so, so if he's on my lap for a scratch it is imperative to recognize his body language. This way I can tell when he's ready to poo and put him in an appropriate place before it's too late. I always check my clothing after I've been handling him – the probability of poopage is always high! (I often think the frequency of poopage is directly related to the cost of the clothing you're wearing).

Another thing birds do is keep their beaks clean. I'm sure you've seen birds removing bits of food by wiping their beaks on whatever they're perching on. Dorian will do this too, on his perch or a tablecloth or my leg or whatever is close by.

He keeps HIMSELF tidy – the rest of the world is its own problem.

HOW TO PERFORM BEAKY-WIPE

After eating something especially messy, like mashed potatoes or grits or whipped cream, Dorian's beak is the most amazing (and rather funny-looking) mess you can imagine. Being basically a clean animal, he'll want to tidy up his beak and if you're not quick enough he'll wipe his beak onto the TV table or the arm of the sofa. This is why we recommend either feeding him only on his play stand or in his cage, or if you big-heartedly invite him to the table with you to dine off your plate, I recommend two precautions.

First, put a large napkin under him to catch the food he'll inevitably throw and

Secondly, keep a quick eye on the condition of his beak and give him "beaky-wipe" as often as needed. Here's how it's done:

Take a dry cloth napkin, facial tissue, washcloth or whatever non-scratchy material you have that does NOT have any cleaning liquid on it

(moist towelettes are NOT a good choice) and TELL HIM you're going to give him beaky-wipe. Always keep in mind that birds do NOT like surprises! Now, there's a game we play with Dorian that involves napkins so if it's beaky-wipe time he needs to know you're not going to play with him – you're going to clean him up. With one hand, gently hold the back of his head and use the other hand to wipe his beak with the cloth. This can usually be done with one gentle motion but two "swipes" is not unusual.

Here's an important part of beaky-wipe that must not be overlooked. Once you've done your beaky-wipe you need to offer Dorian a clean edge of the cloth so he can clean the inner edge of his upper beak (maxillary rost…oh, you know). He'll do this by taking the edge of the napkin into his mouth and you'll see him rub it against his beak. He is NOT eating the napkin, he's cleaning himself.

If he's really been making a mess of himself or has been eating something sticky, he'll need Beaky-Wash, which is simply beaky-wipe with a WET cloth.

Oh, and it isn't unusual for Dorian to ASK for beaky-wipe or beaky-wash and he'll frequently talk about having a dirty beaky or being a dirty birdy, though a quick examination of his face will tell you whether he means it or is just playing with the phrases.

BATH TIME!

No doubt you've heard or read about people taking a plant mister and giving their birds a lovely, gentle bath. Rover and Polgara just love to be bathed this way – they'll spread their wings open and make contented little clucking noises during mist-baths and sometimes they'll try to get in front of one another to get the MOST water all over them. They can't get enough bath time and will stand in front of the mister until they're absolutely soaked to the skin – which would be LONG after both Al's and my wrists have given out – spraying repeatedly is great exercise but one can only do it for so long.

Dorian is different – of course. While I bathe the other birds Dorian looks on with disgust while he carefully moves to the part of his cage furthest away from the spray. But don't think he prefers to stay dirty – on the contrary; he just prefers to bathe HIS WAY. This consists of doing a sort of splashy dance in his water dish, and the colder the water the better he likes it. This often gets more water on the carpet below the cage than on the bird but he definitely prefers it that way and will repeat "Want more bath" until I've refilled his water dish for the fifty-seventh time (I exaggerate – it only FEELS like fifty-seven refills) and he's gotten most of himself and a lot of the carpet soaking wet. I can't help but wonder if he learned this behavior from Rover, who splashes in his water dish AFTER his spray-bath. Rover also takes water into his large beak and throws it into the air so it lands on his back...and the cage and the floor and me but thankfully

Dorian hasn't picked up this habit. In either case I find myself drying out the carpet a lot but at least the birds are clean.

Another way birds keep themselves clean and tidy is by preening.

PREENING – WHAT IT'S REALLY ABOUT

Feathers are actually very sophisticated structures and birds spend a great deal of time every day maintaining them. There are several types of feathers on every bird, from their long flight feathers to the soft, fluffy down next to their skin. There are many functions that feathers perform such as (obviously) flight and providing warmth, contour, aerodynamic efficiency and steering ability.

Some of Dorian's various feathers

Birds from different areas of the world have different types of feathers that are best suited for life in their particular habitat. For example, my three birds each come from different continents and their feathers reflect the differences in their natural habitats.

Rover, the Umbrella Cockatoo, is indigenous to the Australian desert, and has fewer feathers than my other two birds. His feathers are loosely packed and he is one of the species called Powder Down birds; birds that have specialized down feathers that shed a fine, wax-like powder instead of preening oil. This powder waterproofs his feathers, maintains their smoothness and helps keep him cool in his naturally hot, dry climate.

Rover's white wing feather, 2 of Polgara's wing feathers, and one of Dorian's.

Polgara is from the Amazon jungle in South America. She has the most feathers of my three, and they are very densely packed. She exudes an oil to lubricate her wings which keeps them waterproof – something important to a bird whose home turf is a rain forest.

Dorian's feather fall between the others' – he's from central Africa where it's hot but it rains seasonally. He's doesn't have as many feathers as Polgara, though he does have more than Rover.

Also like Rover, Dorian is a Powder Down bird with the same sort of specialized down feathers that produce quite a quantity of powder. In fact, Dorian (and most African Greys) produces so much powder that if you lift one of his wings and blow beneath it across his body you'll see a fine cloud of powder; a process our daughter calls "dusting the bird."

As a side note, people with dust allergies and certain respiratory difficulties may be irritated by this bird-produced powder, though perhaps in recompense, petting a Powder Down bird feels much softer and silkier than petting other bird species.

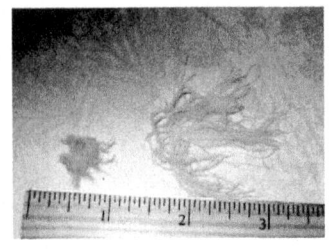
Dorian's small down feather vs Rover's huge one.

No matter where they're from, feathers only last so long and eventually they break down and fall out or are plucked out to be replaced. When birds lose old feathers we call it molting, and it happens once or twice a year or more, depending on the species. I've read some articles online that assert that the time of year a bird molts has to do with their habitat as well as the amount of light available to them. Because our birds live indoors they never really stop molting all year long. There's never a day when I'm not picking up feathers or bits of down from one bird or another. At some times they molt more than at others, and during these intervals I think I could build an extra bird with the large number of feathers on the floor. Feathers are molted symmetrically by the way – if two feathers molt off one wing, the same two will molt off the other wing, which allows the bird to continue flying without having to compensate on one side or the other.

I think the most frequently molted type of feather is the soft down that lies next to birds' skin. I say this because while I might go for a week without finding a molted contour feather

I find down feathers (which we refer to as "bird fluff") every single day and since they're very light and soft they float all over the house so I find them everywhere and in everything.

IMPORTANT STUFF – PAY ATTENTION!

Growing new feathers is no picnic. They emerge from the bird's skin covered in a white sheath of keratin, called a quill.

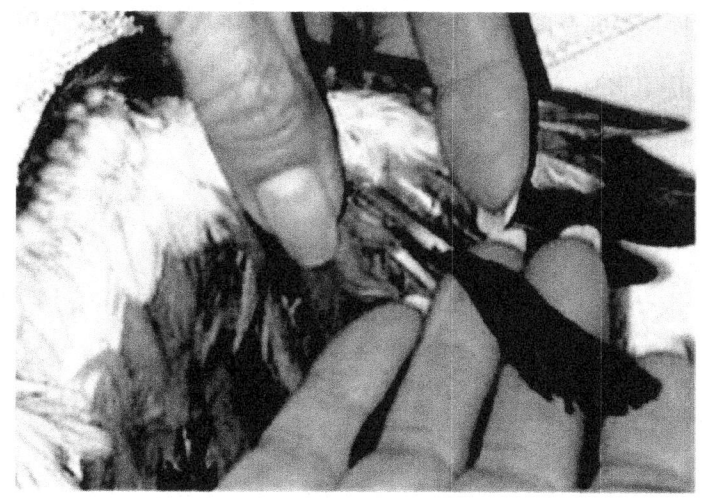

Note the dark bottom and white top of the quill sheath that covers the still-growing feather.
Photo courtesy of All Creatures Veterinarian Care Center, Sewell, NJ

The quill provides very important protection for the new feather (called a pin feather or a blood feather) because during its growth there's a blood vessel inside it which aids in the growth and maturation of the feather. The bottom of the quill remains dark in color as long as blood is flowing within it. If this sheath is broken near the blood vessel the feather **will bleed copiously** and either the feather should be immediately removed as close to the skin as possible and the area staunched until clotting can occur, or the bird should be RUSHED to the nearest avian vet who will remove the feather for you. Yes, they can lose enough blood through a broken blood feather to die!

As each feather matures the blood vessel retracts and the keratin sheath begins to flake away. There's a wonderful article about blood feathers that you can read online thanks to *All Creatures Veterinarian Care Center* in Sewell, NJ. The URL for this article is:

http://allcreaturesvetcare.com/exotic_search.php?category=&id=434

CAUTION: Newly emerged quills are VERY sensitive – imagine having a group of pencils coming out of your skin, each with the sharpened tip pointing toward your flesh. All you need is for someone to brush up against you and these pencils will poke you quite painfully. That's what it's like for birds with new feathers growing in. If you touch a quill in the wrong way it HURTS and many a bite has been the result of a mistaken touch!

At the same time, as the feathers mature, the birds preen more actively to crack open the disintegrating quills and let the new feathers uncurl and grow out completely. When you see a bird preening around the back of another bird's head what you're looking at is one bird cracking those quills for the other bird. Dorian, having no other mate but me (resigned sigh), often puts his head down when he's growing new feathers so I can crack open the quills for him. There's an inherent danger in this: if they're still dark and thick they need to be left alone – they're still blood feathers and dangerous to fool with. If they tend to crack easily I do my best to gently pinch or scrape at them. This is a delicate process and if I had a dollar for every time I've gotten bitten because I hurt Dorian unintentionally when doing this for him I'd be driving a Rolls Royce!

As you can see, preening is an everyday chore and includes not only the feathers but even the feet and talons.

🦜 MORNING IS FLOCK TIME

Al and our flock – on his shoulders just for the photograph!

We mentioned earlier that every morning birds call out to the world, announcing their presence in the neighborhood. Another flock-member identifier Dorian uses in the mornings is to call out half a musical phrase, (such as the first note of a wolf-whistle) and wait for one of us to answer with the second half. This reassures him that we're still "present in the flock" if we're in a room where he can't see us.

Now that Al and I are present all day long a pattern of behavior has firmly established itself. Mornings are the time for chosen flock members to stay together. Usually this means that if Al and I are working in our shared office, Dorian absolutely MUST be in the room with us. Sometimes this involves petting, preening, or multiple bird journeys across my keyboard however for the most part all he wants is to be in the same room with us. And be petted. And eat our breakfast. And get petted some more. Actually, just sitting quietly on the T-stand is often an acceptable activity, too. He'll sit and watch us or preen or rest, but eventually he'll get bored. If we're lucky this means he'll jump down onto the seed catcher level of the T-stand and quietly tear strips of the lining newspaper and drop them to the floor. If he's in a more demanding mood he'll jump onto my keyboard drawer for scratching, petting, keyboard-surfing or generally getting in the way. The point is, in the mornings he needs to be with us. If we put him in his cage in the other room he'll peep insistently or, like a prisoner holding the bars of his cell in an old movie, he'll call out repeatedly – "wanna come out! Wanna come out!"

AFTERNOON IS NAP TIME

Once the morning hubbub is over and we've given Dorian the attention, worship, and petting or preening he feels is his due, he settles down to a nice snack (elevensies? Second Breakfast?) in his cage. Keeping in mind that as flock animals, the birds always wish to be with other members of the flock, it always seems to be an issue of mild anxiety if Dorian cannot see us, even though he knows quite certainly that we're still in the house. His having spent a few hours in the office with us seems to allay these concerns and he stays fairly quiet and contented in his cage, playing with his toys, looking out the window for anything interesting, talking to himself or taking the required afternoon nap.

Rover taking a nap beside Polgara

All three of our birds tend to nap in the afternoon, usually some time between two and four pm. Their naps vary in length, and while, like all prey animals, they're easily awakened, sometimes they are able to nap again after whatever excitement woke them in the first place. The best sign that they're about to nap is a behavior called beak scraping or beak grinding. They quietly scrape their lower beak (mandibular…oh, never mind) against their upper, which is an indication of relaxation and contentment, and you can pretty well predict that, barring sudden noises or distractions, Fluffie-Wuffums is about to go nappy-time. Often they'll also puff their feathers out slightly, and sometimes they'll raise one foot. They won't always put their heads on their backs at nap time, though they invariably do this at bedtime in the evenings.

An interesting thing I've noticed is their respect for other creatures' naps. If they're raucously playing with a jingly ball or triumphantly announcing that they've once more defeated the plastic foraging toy by perching upside down on it and batting it with their beaks, if they see Al or me lying down on the sofa for a late afternoon snooze they very soon quiet down and ~~read a book~~ go for a snack or preen their feet or just plain watch us sleep. Sometimes they'll decide they could use another nap themselves.

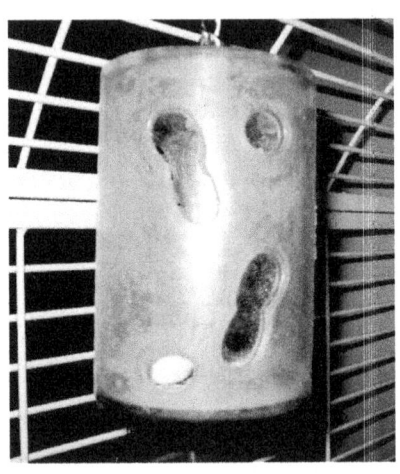

Dorie's favorite plastic foraging toy

Ordinarily they'll let us sleep as long as we wish however they watch us carefully, and at the very first sign of consciousness they'll start chattering or chirping, and Dorian will of course demand his fair share by asking either to be let out of his cage or for a food treat.

IS HE SCHIZOPHRENIC DURING BREEDING TIME? WELL, YES AND NO!

An excellent article in Feathered Family, Inc, which is a parrot rescue and adoption facility in Colorado, outlines parrot behavior during breeding season; the time during which it's most likely Dorian will bite hard enough to draw blood. It can be found here:

http://www.featheredfamily.com/parrothormones.htm

African Greys are one of the several parrot species known to breed all year long. This doesn't mean that they're constantly "hormonal", it means they're prone to reacting to an environment that mimics spring breeding times. It's actually normal that Dorian suddenly goes from "Sweetness-and-Cherry-Pie-Bappy-Bird" to "Ivan-the-Seriously-Terrible-With-A-Bit-Of-Dracula-Thrown-In". These times occur rather abruptly and are signaled by suddenly protective and territorial behavior which is fairly easy to miss unless you're actually on the active lookout. Out of nowhere Dorian will start to bite the hands that feed and pet him (quite literally). This is very trying, both physically (as you watch your abrupt blood-loss) and emotionally, as all you were doing was innocently petting and adoring him. Actually, touching the bird during this period can be misinterpreted ("No, Dorie, you are I are just GOOD FRIENDS!"). All you want on your (bleeding) hands is an over-stimulated bird who thinks you wanted more than just a cuddle – and even if you had seriously off-the-charts proclivities and wanted to "do your feathered friend a favor", you're certainly not equipped for the job!

How do you figure out that he's in breeding mode? He may become territorial, moody, and prone to biting, and only after a day or two (when you've already begun to think he needs a generous injection of Prozac) will he start to regurgitate food for his chosen mate (you lucky person!). Believe me; it's best NOT to encourage this behavior but at the same time it would be a mistake to punish him for "doing what comes naturally". He won't understand it.

Thankfully, there are a few things you can do to minimize this trying time which can last for several days to a few weeks. First, limit the starches and sugars he eats because they increase his hormones. Don't feed him warm, mushy food, which is reminiscent of what he regurgitates as part of courtship behavior – he may think *you're* courting *him*. Only pet him in non-sexual areas like the tops of his wings. Minimize his exposure to sunlight and make sure he gets at least 12 hours of darkness (hopefully he'll sleep the entire 12 hours).

How old will Dorian be when he finally becomes "geriatric" and stops going through these hormonal intervals? It's very difficult to say. Some articles say that once an African Grey is over 20 he's reached middle age, while others insist that they age at pretty much the same rate we do, and can still be sexually active at 40 or older!

🐦 TOYS AND OTHER AMUSEMENTS

Like human children, every bird enjoys different kinds of toys and games. Dorian prefers shredding paper (newspaper is the favored material) and hanging upside-down to attack his plastic toys. He has no interest in playing with balls by himself, though he'll chase a "jingle ball" if we're actively playing with him. Since he often says "Here!" when he wants us to give him something, we call this game "Here" because when he wants the ball, he'll call for it. He does not favor plastic chain toys or foraging boxes, though he's recently developed an interest in rope toys.

Typical rope toy for birds

Polgara, on the other hand (actually I should say, "other foot") simply loves balls with jingle bells in them, and will hold one and shake it for prolonged periods of time. This is no surprise, given her proclivity for singing along with opera – she's a true music lover. She also enjoys pushing cowbells until they clang – an activity I'm only able to tolerate for short periods of time. Anything that makes a sound is her favorite thing.

Rover, being an enormously intelligent bird, loves rope toys because once he bites off the bits of wood and unties the bits of plastic (yes, unties. I meant it.) he takes the strings of rope and ties them around selected bars of the cage. During our trip across the country I had put a rope toy in 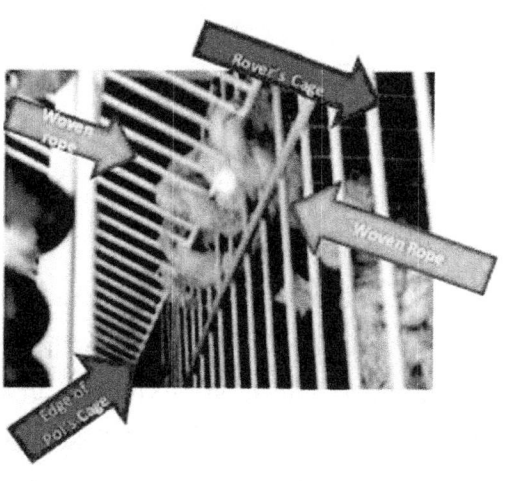 Rover's travel cage, and he carefully tied his cage to Polgara's. Adorable as well as startlingly smart!

Rover also enjoys biting little bits of cloth out of towels or his cage cover and jamming them between his food bowl and the metal rim that holds it. I can only imagine he does this to try to prevent my removing the bowl every morning. That's just my impression because sometimes he tries to grab the bowl from me in the morning despite the fact that I've been returning it freshly filled for over 25 years. I have no idea what he REALLY means by this trick – I only know he does it all the time. In fact, we've relinquished ownership of his favorite towel to him and he arranges it and bites it and moves it around to his heart's content. He also loves to create caves and nests with it. Once created, he "stocks" the 'cave/nest' with toys and bits of food. Rover loves putting things into containers and taking them out again. A bit obsessive-compulsive but it's his thing. Rover also loves chewing up cardboard boxes and anything at all made of wood, including the perches he stands on. In fact, if Long John Silver had actually owned a parrot, chances are good the bird would have snuck down every night while Long John was asleep and made matchsticks out of that wooden leg!

Interactive games are Dorie's favorites. Something he'll do which is natural behavior in birds is to sing half a musical theme, such as the first half of a wolf whistle (we mentioned this earlier). He expects and is waiting for me or Al to finish the musical phrase. In the wild, birds do this to locate other flock members and we believe this is why Dorian does it, too.

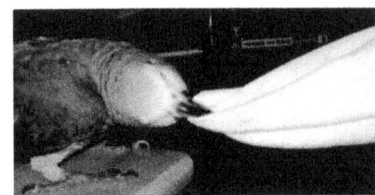

Another game he enjoys is to take the tip of a napkin in his beak and pull it from side to side and then up and down while whichever human is playing with him makes the noises and whistles he associates with this game. This can get fairly funny when he

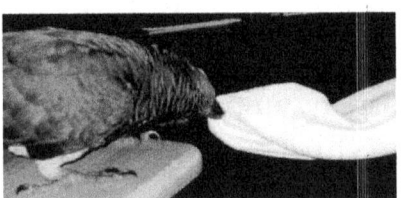

bobs his head up and down so quickly it becomes impossible to whistle fast enough to keep up. I think that's his favorite part of this game.

"Tickle Time" is also an occasional favorite in which Dorian will say "tickle the bird" and if you approach him with your fingers he'll lift up a wing so you can tickle him beneath it. He doesn't appear to get any particular giggles or sensation of tickling, since one tickles his feathers and not his skin but he likes the interaction.

Dorian also enjoys word games. Like so many young humans, he loves to play "Peek-A-Boo", in which we cover him entirely with a cloth napkin or small towel and ask, "Where's Dorian?" Once we pull off the cover he'll happily say "Peek-A-Boo!" He is entirely aware that this game has

to do with someone hiding. Sometimes if he's in his cage and Al and I are busy in the office we don't reply to his calls for attention, and he'll tug at my heart-strings by calling out "Peek-A-Boo!" as though he's hoping to make us suddenly appear.

This game had a startling conclusion one day. While our daughter was in high school Al would drive there every afternoon to pick her

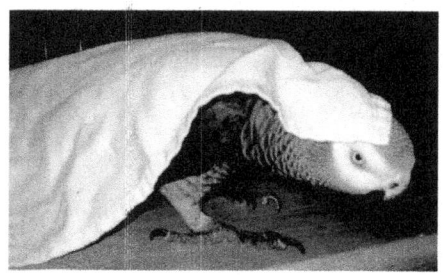

up after classes, and most days he brought Dorian with him. (This was the era when young Dorian learned to eagerly say "go for a ride in the car?"). Once Rachael got into the car she'd take the bird onto her hand and pet him and chat and play with him on the ride home. Part of this playtime often included the "Peek-A-Boo" game, during which Rachael would put her shirt or sweater over the bird before saying, "Where's Dorian?" One particular day she had covered him in this manner and said, "Where's Dorian?" to which the bird replied, "Where's Rachael?"

Another of his favorite games is "Time to Bonk the Bird on the Beak." Sometimes he'll ask to play this game by saying "Bonk the Bird on the Beak." We sing the phrase while gently tapping the tip of his beak with a finger or any small object we might be holding.

"Birdy In The Bag" is another grand amusement. First you take a paper grocery bag and tear a small hole in the bottom of it. Then place Dorian and the bag on the floor with the opening of the bag facing him. Station yourself on the far side of the grocery bag and put your finger slightly through the hole and make scratchy noises on the bag. Dorian will crouch down into "stalking position" and enter the bag and at this point have your reflexes ready because the bird will leap forward to catch "the worm" (i.e. your finger!) that's

Dorian inside the bag looking out

sticking its head through that little hole in the bottom of the bag. This game amuses him mightily and as long as you're brave enough to put a finger through that hole he'll try repeatedly to catch it. Be careful – this IS a biting game!

Early on I mentioned that our daughter Rachael can do things with Dorian neither Al nor I can safely attempt. One of these activities is a game called "Bat Bird" in which she holds him by the feet and turns him upside down so he's suspended like a bat. Now, those who remember the old Adam West "Batman" television series will know what I'm talking about when I tell you that once the bird is hanging upside down Rachael or Dorian will sing "Bat Bird! -do-do-do-do-do-do-do-do-do!'; the musical theme from that old TV show. Al and I can play that game verbally but neither of us dare attempt holding him upside down by the feet.

Another activity enjoyed by birds everywhere is singing. This not only provides necessary communication, it's also fun. We know that birds call to one another to ascertain where each of the flock members are. We humans do that sort of thing, too ("Johnny, are you out in the back yard?" "Yeah, mom." "What are you doing?" "Nothing" "Is Sarah with you?" "Yeah." "Sarah, what are you doing?" "Me and Johnny are burying the cash we took from Dad's wallet.").

We sing songs for many reasons, some of which are for play or to help learn things. We've been very impressed by videos of parrots successfully singing entire songs completely in tune so we were eager to try this out ourselves. What we discovered was that our African Grey Parrot can't carry a tune! We might never have learned this if we simply imitated the whistles he's invented however when we were "at the helm" the awful truth came out. I can't help but wonder if the reason he's so good at imitating sounds, words, and phrases is because he can't sing very well. That's not to say he doesn't enjoy it – he sings and chatters all through the day, though you sometimes have to already know which tune he's singing in order to recognize it. For example, we taught him a little song that we sing to the tune of "Frère Jacques" which goes,

Hello, Duck-bird, Hello Duck-bird
How are you? How are you?
Happy Little Duck-Bird, Happy Little Duck-bird
Quack Quack Quack, Quack Quack Quack

Dorie will often sing this song when he's by himself however he rarely sings the words entirely in the correct order and he never, ever follows the tune correctly. He usually comes out with "Hello Duck-bird, Happy the Duck-bird – QUACK!". Absolutely tone deaf to this one but his version is still adorable.

Another song we've been trying to teach him for years and years is "Jingle Bells." We not only sing this song to him, we whistle it, because he seems to find it easier to discover and repeat a tune in whistles. He can repeat some of the musical phrases correctly in whistles, though never in their proper order, and as usual, you already have to know the tune to recognize which part of it he's trying to repeat. Sometimes he uses Jingle Bells as a locator phrase, where he'll whistle the first part and wait to hear us finish the musical phrase so he knows where we are. As to the words, the closest he's ever gotten to singing it accurately was "Jingle Bell. Jingle Way. Oh, what a good bird!" I thought it was an improvement over the original, actually.

Toys for birds come in all shapes, sizes, and materials. They can be found in most pet stores, some veterinarian offices, farmers' markets, and occasionally grocery stores, though the latter usually only carry toys for small birds, such as parakeets, finches, and canaries. I've found that a lot of dog toys are appropriate for birds, especially rope toys, though you should avoid those with objects on them. A bird will invariably chew on anything attached to a toy and may injure himself or eat an inappropriate object. Many years ago Rover discovered the joys of biting apart small "jingle balls" but when he reached the jingle bell at the center he bit into it right at the bottom opening and got it stuck on his beak. It took us an hour to remove it! Oh, and when the bird has done a good job pulling a rope toy apart it should be REMOVED from the cage because the individual strings that make up the rope can get tangled around feet or toes and cut off blood circulation! Be careful to watch for this – a bird CAN lose toes to this!

One final note about bird toys. Some of them, especially those made of or including acrylic plastic, can be very expensive. If you wrap up such a toy in a nice cardboard box and present it to "Wingums", don't be awfully surprised if, just like a small human child, the bird ignores the expensive toy in favor of playing endlessly with the box it came in.

THE MOUTH AND THE FOOT ARE THE HANDS

Well, think about it. Birds don't have hands per se; their hands are busy being wings, so everything you and I do with our hands, birds do with their mouths or their feet. Their extraordinary ability to balance on one foot while delicately holding a piece of food (probably from your plate) in the other is something I've always admired. But there's far, far more to it than that.

Dorian really enjoys meatballs

THE MOUTH

Naturally, most people are afraid to allow their fingers to go into a bird's mouth. This is actually a mistake for the most part, though admittedly, getting seriously bitten is certainly a possibility. The easiest way to get hurt, however, is to pull your hand back when a bird wants to take your finger into its mouth. Usually they're just exploring who you are, or greeting you in an avian fashion.

Oftentimes if you pull your hand back it's really you hurting yourself because if you think about it you'll realize that the bird hasn't actually bitten you; he's just squeezed a bit. Believe me; a parrot's beak is VERY strong. I've read that they can exert over 200 pounds of pressure per square inch with their beaks. Many, many years ago Al and I saw an angry Blue-Fronted Amazon parrot chomp through an inch-and-three-quarter piece of oak dowel in one bite! With this in mind, understand that even if you get bitten, the bird is quite carefully not exerting its strength. If it did you might actually lose that finger! Since parrots are not hunters, they have few reasons to deliberately separate you from your digits unless they feel seriously threatened.

Dorian will sometimes acknowledge a favor or treat (i.e. say "thank you") by taking your finger into his mouth and giving it a little squeeze BEFORE he takes the treat from you. Admittedly, this can be annoying or startling because he doesn't do it every time however it's just an acknowledgement, not an attack.

Their lack of hands probably contributes to the fact that they will chew on anything and everything; partly to see how it feels and tastes, partly to find out if it's edible, and partly because it's fun to do so.

One behavior of note is that birds sometimes greet one another by touching each other's tongues. If you haven't leaned down and offered your tongue to a bird it'll assume your finger will do the job instead and will take your fingertip into its mouth and explore it with its tongue.

THE FEET

Anything that isn't explored with the mouth is investigated with the feet. Birds' feet are wonderfully dexterous. Rover likes to eat tiny safflower seeds by placing them one at a time on his foot and delicately eating it. As you can see from the photo of Dorie holding a meatball a few pages back, holding food is the easiest thing in the world, and this is true from tiny things like sunflower seeds to toys to tools. Yes, our birds use tools, too. Nothing sophisticated you understand; just simple things like the time Dorian held a small spoon in his foot to feed himself ice cream.

COMBINED EFFORTS

Sometimes they will combine the use of their mouths and feet to accomplish their aims. When Rover plays with his favorite towel, cramming it into the space between his bowl and the metal rim that holds it, he'll use a combination of foot and mouth; anchoring the heavy towel with a foot while he manipulates the cloth carefully with his mouth. That's also how he tied together his and Polgara's travel cage when we crossed the country. Using his mouth, feet and wings in a concerted effort was how he successfully caught our vertical blinds when we thought we'd moved his cage far enough that they'd be out of his reach.

SO DON'T KID YOURSELF; YOU WILL BE BITTEN!

Since it's inevitable that your finger(s) will eventually end up in the bird's mouth we really should tell you that there's a right way and a wrong way to present your digits so they don't get hurt. It's the same thing you'd do if you want the bird to climb onto your hand. You wouldn't point your fingertips at the bird; you'd hold your hand perpendicular to his feet so he can step up. In the same way, when your finger is near his mouth you need to keep it perpendicular to his beak. In this way your favorite digit can be inserted PAST the sharp tip of his upper beak (maxillary…yeah). If your finger is pointed at his beak there's hardly any way he can avoid pressing that sharp tip against your flesh, whether he wants to or not.

So why does he bite? Sometimes Dorian just wants to warn you off and will give you a little bite which is really no more than his taking your finger into his mouth and holding on to it (I personally find this somewhat unnerving). If you hurt him, say, when you're trying to crack open quills on his neck and accidently poke him with one of them, he'll "even the score" by twisting his head and giving you a warning bite, as though to say, "That HURT! Watch it!" He doesn't usually break the skin when he does this but it DOES hurt.

Then there are the times that he's angry or hormonal and just plain CHOMPS down on you. Often this will draw blood, and if he's really angry and definitely wants to hurt you he'll actually say, "OW!" as he's crunching down on you. At these times you need to understand that even when he's hurting you he's being very considerate! I can hear your incredulity as you read that but you have to keep in mind that parrots' beaks are VERY strong — they're capable of biting entirely through your finger if they needed to (picture Dorian in his native Africa crunching through a zebra bone to get to the marrow). Luckily for us though, parrots' aggression is mostly defensive so they're not likely to exert their full strength because they've suddenly decided you'd make a nice meal. Nope, not going to happen. They're opportunists, not killers.

Keep in mind that being handled and petted is NOT natural to birds; especially by a creature they're aware is a predator. Sometimes they just want to be in the room with us but they don't want to be handled. If they look like they're going to bite your tender, loving fingers, they probably will. Don't take it personally; they're just not in the mood. Hey, I'm the same way sometimes.

WHY WE STICK-TRAINED THE BIRDS

It's very simple. Sometimes I want to transport Dorian to somewhere he doesn't want to go. If I pick him up onto my fingers, when I get to the destination he'll clutch my hand like a vise and will NOT let go until I move him to someplace he'd rather be. This can become painful (and bloody, if his talons haven't been trimmed), beside increasing the likelihood that if he gets annoyed with my insisting he goes where he doesn't want to go he'll reach down between his feet and bite me (yes, it's happened). He and I both know that if he's on a stick he MUST get down no matter the destination because:

1) if he doesn't I will roll the stick until he does.

2) he can't hurt the stick by clutching tightly onto it.

3) the stick won't complain or care if he bites it, and neither will I.

This is even more true with our Amazon parrot, Polgara. Amazons are very assertive birds who want what they want WHEN they want it and she has no qualms about biting whenever she feels it necessary. Also, though she gets along with Al she actually doesn't like me (even though I'm the one who feeds her and saves her from Rover's over-enthusiasm every day). She expresses this by threatening me every time I approach. As well, she doesn't happily tolerate my touching her so our relationship is carried on primarily at stick-length.

Oh, but don't think these birds step up automatically any time I present them with the stick. If they don't want to get up both Dorian and Polgara will put their beak down between their feet and the stick, as though running interference so I can't get the stick near enough for them to step up. They can be pretty persistent about this, but then again – so can I!

To be truthful, Rover the cockatoo will not step onto a stick for any reason. He will happily bite it or push it around the cage but under no circumstances have we ever gotten him to stand on one. Part of the problem might be that the dowels we use are 3/8" and are really too small for Rover's very large feet however attempts made with thicker dowels have also been unsuccessful. Luckily, where Polgara goes, Rover will go and he'll readily jump up onto my or Al's arm to follow her to the playpen. This too can be painful as his talons grow long and needle-sharp very quickly and sometimes just having him stand on your arm can result in small lacerations.

WHEN THE CAT'S AWAY THE BIRD WILL PLAY

Any and every time you turn your back the bird will attempt to do something you've already forbidden. Blazing trails to new territories, such as your delicate lace tablecloth or the grandfather clock you inherited from your great great grandfather is a constant occupation, which explains why we never leave Dorian alone in a room for more than a minute at a time. (These occasional minutes are usually taken to stop the two other birds from arguing or sparring with each other).

The point is that birds have no idea that you'd rather they didn't bite holes in the furniture or happily chew the 'Escape' button off your keyboard. Their curiosity and playfulness NEVER ends and despite understanding what you mean by "NO!" they will ALWAYS make yet another attempt to eat those exciting and colorful pieces of the jigsaw puzzle you're working on in the dining room. No, they cannot see the "big picture" (pun entirely intended). Lacking our unique sense of the passage of time, Dorian believes that when you say, "Do NOT climb up onto the mailman!" you mean it just for that instant, and once he has graciously obeyed and gone back to his perch (thus proving what a good bird he is) he feels perfectly welcome to immediately attempt to climb back up onto the terrified postal worker.

This is also true of aggressive behavior, by the way. Adult male cockatoos have a tendency toward violence with other birds, and our Rover has more than once hurt Polgara in his enthusiasm to somehow occupy the same space she's occupying. That and the fact that he does NOT share things leads to daily arguments, tiffs, and downright skirmishes between those two. In fact they can go from sweet cuddling with Rover's big, white wing lovingly over Polgara's shoulder to angry bloodshed in less time than it takes for a feather to drop to the floor.

OBEDIENCE – OR – YOU THINK HERDING CATS IS HARD?

One always needs to keep in mind that though a bird may understand what you're instructing it to do, this is not at all the same thing as OBEYING. Training a bird is NOT like training a dog. It isn't a matter of "Now you know not to go up onto the couch so I never have to worry about your doing that ever again." Oh no. Birds, believing they are the center of the universe, will obey what you tell them to do as long as it goes along with what the bird itself wants to do. Birds will ALWAYS attempt to do anything they want to do.

A dog will always obey your command to "sit" because it looks to you as its pack leader and it knows there's benefit in following your orders. Flocks don't operate like that; especially since the flock leader can change from one minute to the next. As prey animals they're aware that any situation can change at any moment. Though it may please "Firebird" to comply with your nervous instruction to get off that Fabergé egg your Great Aunt Tatiana sent to you from Russia, he will always assume you told him to do so because there might be a momentary danger associated with his sitting on it. It won't ever occur to him that the danger might come from you wanting to pluck his feathers out if he destroys it, by the way. If you're lucky, hey'll obey you because he believe it's in his interest to do so – maybe you'll hand him a treat for obeying. But situations change, so once "Firebird" has done your bidding he'll naturally feel free to perch up there again. He'll never understand why you get frustrated about this. His mind simply doesn't work that way.

Here's a more realistic example (because I don't know anyone who owns a real Fabergé egg). Dorian likes to stand on my keyboard drawer whenever I'm at my computer. This drawer is on a lower level than the desk and I always have important papers up there. Dorie is always eager to climb up and explore the desk but when I remove him and tell him not to go there again he'll obey…for about a second. Then he'll climb up again, and the scenario is repeated ad nauseam until I remove him to his T-stand. Now, I'm sure he knows I don't want him there because before he jumps up he'll say things that show he expects my disapproval like, "No, Dorie. No up. Bad Birdie." This awareness of my opinion has never once influenced his jumping up onto my desk.

Birds most certainly can be trained to respond in certain ways when they're rewarded with a food treat or are taught to respond to a "clicker" but always keep in mind that their focus is the treat, not the behavior, or making you especially happy.

Does this mean your birdie doesn't love you? No, it doesn't mean that at all. It simply means their focus is inward, to their own agenda, not outward, to yours.

THE MOST DIFFICULT CONCEPTS TO TEACH A BIRD

The first is the concept of time. The closest birds get to telling time is their appreciation of the location of the sun. Daylight indicates time to get up and sunset means it's time to settle down. Don't ever rely on a bird to remind you when your favorite TV show is on – guaranteed you'll miss it.

A good example of this is that birds don't differentiate between breakfast, lunch, dinner or suppertime – eating is eating and in the wild they do it as often as the opportunity arises. This explains why Dorie calls for "dinner" early in the morning. The word means "food" or "eating" to him – there's no desire or need for him to differentiate one meal from another; especially according to the time of day.

He'll often say "good night" instead of "good morning" when he first comes out of his sleeping box however he never mixes up those two expressions when he's ready to go to bed in the evening. At that time it's always either "good night" or "wanna go to bedtime".

Our telling him that we'll "be back soon" has no definite meaning either. He's learned that when we say "I'll be right back" the duration will be very brief, and when we let him know we're "going for a ride in the car" he expects us to be gone for a long while but for no specific duration.

Another really difficult concept for our birds to comprehend is the fact that their actions have consequences. Every time Dorian has seriously bitten one of us he gets sternly reprimanded and sent for a "time out" into his sleeping box however this has never stopped him. The same is true of his peeping in his shrill, "I want attention NOW" voice. It isn't as though he doesn't realize it annoys us – he does. Perhaps his need for attention outweighs his desire to stay in our good graces?

Another example of this lack of understanding is that Rover will chew through the perch he's standing on, despite the fact that the last three times he did the same thing he plummeted to the bottom of the cage when he bit through (yes, just like in the old cartoons). Does the fun of chewing up the perch outweigh the bad experience of falling down or does he just not understand that A+B=C?

A particularly annoying lack of understanding concerns the concept that WANTING something does not guarantee OBTAINING it. I believe this is a large bone of contention between many, many humans who live with companion birds. Birds appear to think in absolutes where wanting something is concerned. A good example of this is when Dorian wants to come out of his cage but we want him to stay inside it. He will endlessly repeat "Wanna come out", interspersed with attention-getting peeps, as though he seriously believes that for some reason we're not hearing the request but will certainly fulfill it as soon as we catch on that he wants something. Rover and Polgara do the same thing, though since they don't speak English it's a little more difficult to figure out what all the shouting is about. They don't appear to understand that their request might not be honored. Eventually they'll get bored or distracted and stop the demand but enduring the long-term calling until they give up is the reason we keep a good supply of ear plugs in strategic places all around the house. No, really. We do.

Generally speaking, any non-concrete concept is very difficult to teach, at least in our house. Dorian's very good with words to which he can directly relate however concepts about things outside his ability to experience them seem to be beyond his understanding. Like "attention." If Dorian wants our attention he'll call repeatedly for food or to come out of his cage. Though we've offered the word "attention" to him he's never picked it up. It appears that he does not or cannot think in abstracts where his desires are concerned. Perhaps they're too urgent for him to think out.

I've also tried to get him to say "I love you" but without great success. He's sort of said a non-committal version of the phrase but I don't think he understood what he was imitating. I've heard that a lot of birds do use the phrase – I'm still waiting for that magical moment with Dorie.

THE MOST DIFFICULT CONCEPTS TO TEACH A BIRD OWNER

The first concept is something I sometimes have difficulty remembering myself. In the morning just after Dorian has eaten breakfast he'll invariably call out that he wants to come out of his cage. If I don't respond quickly enough to suit him he'll make piercing peep and chirp sounds, interspersed with other phrases and requests, such as "want kiwi", "want apple" and so forth. The concept one has to keep in mind is that at these times he doesn't really want more food – he's just eaten. What he wants, as previously mentioned, is attention. The fact that I may not want or be able to give him my attention has no bearing whatsoever on his behavior. Like very young humans, birds are not usually able to look outside their own needs and wants, so your needs are never considered. Plus, they are extremely TENACIOUS in demanding what they want – to the point that it can drive you to distraction. ("Dorian, >SOB< it's all about YOUR needs, isn't it!?")

Another concept that's enormously difficult to accept is that the only really effective way to break a screaming habit (in the bird, I mean) is to ignore it. I've read in countless books and articles that when birds make a lot of noise they just adore the drama that unfolds as they watch you shake your fist and scream back at them. These authors are right that when

YOU shout at them you're training them that shouting is an acceptable thing to do, even when you're shouting, "STOP MAKING THAT GODAWFUL NOISE!" Ignoring bad behavior (like ignoring a tantrum in a human child) until your non-response has taken all the fun out of screaming at the top of their lungs is the best way to eventually end this maddening behavior. The HARDEST part is actually retaining your hearing and your sanity while subduing your natural impulse to scream at them as images of torture and dismemberment appear involuntarily in your mind. Training a bird not to scream (called causing the extinction of the behavior) is NOT a quick or a fun process.

Another concept we humans have trouble with is understanding and keeping in mind that birds do not think in the same way we do. Humans do this all the time with everything. It's called "personification". Animation studios and advertising agencies make enormous fortunes creating stories of various animals, plants, cars, robots and what-have-you doing human-type things and thinking in human ways. We need to stop and realize that no other animal on Earth thinks in just the same way we do. This attitude is why we're so startled to see other species doing intelligent things – we judge them by our own values. We all know that dolphins are very intelligent but if you judge them by their ability to build a house you'd think them stupid! I expect that dolphins look at the clumsy way we swim and catch fish and think *we're* pretty stupid.

"SOMEBODY STOP ME – I WANT TO KILL THAT BIRD!!"

Sometimes all the bird wants is to be in the same room with us but he can be so insistent (see the section called "The Most Difficult Concepts to Teach a Bird") that he can make us crazy. Like many birds, if he doesn't immediately get what he wants he calls loudly for attention and he does it in the most painful, piercing voice you can imagine. This makes it nearly impossible to wait until he stops the ear-splitting racket and specifies what he wants in English. It's also very difficult to have perfect timing so he sees you responding to the words and not the peeps; especially when he alternates them, which he has the endearing (!) habit of doing. What makes us imagine "bird-i-cide" at these times is not only the imperious insistence Dorian displays (like an absolute ruler wanting his way) but the fact that the sounds are far, far worse than nails on a blackboard. It literally scrapes at our nerves (not to mention our eardrums), usually when we're about to get onto an important conference call or finish that article that's due in less than an hour. Like we've said before; the human's needs are not considered. Birds don't ever grow beyond their natural egocentrism and sometimes it gets to me or Al but fortunately we've never both been driven to the edge at the same time. Would we be serving "parrot stew" for dinner if we both "lost it" at the same time? No but the thought *has* occurred...

The best, and possibly the only way to stop this noisy and maddening behavior is to DISTRACT the bird. When he starts to peep insistently I sometimes whistle a tune he knows and a great percentage of the time he'll stop peeping and start whistling back, which is a natural bird behavior anyway. To be perfectly frank though, it doesn't always work.

Giving the bird a bath is also very distracting. Rover and Polgara really enjoy getting misted until they're soaked through and look drippy and bedraggled but Dorian despises being misted, so it remains an effective, albeit annoying distraction.

Another good distraction when the birds have decided to fill the house with cacophony is the use of a flashlight on the ceiling. Dialed to a small circle, the birds instinctively look up to watch this potential predator, which often makes them forget what they were shouting about.

Once in a while, if we don't respond to his calling to us, Dorian will provide the response he expects from us. This can be very funny when he peeps insistently, then when we ignore it, he angrily says, "What are you doing? I'M PEEPING!!" Sometimes we can't help just shouting out "BE QUIET" to which Dorian sometimes responds, "Damn Bird!!" It's very hard to stifle our laughter at moments like that.

All my birds seem to know just how far they can push before we get seriously angry. Just like human kids, isn't it?

THE PUNISHMENT NEVER REALLY FITS THE CRIME

It's useful to keep in mind that birds are evolved dinosaurs, and as such have been doing whatever they want to do for about 350 million years. Their every action has a motive, and it's often unclear to us humans what that motive might be; especially when the action hurts our ears or destroys our favorite possessions. The point is that, while they may be aware that some things they do meet with our disapproval or anger, this awareness will very often not do anything to deter the action in the first place. Their prime objective isn't to please us; it's to accomplish whatever they have in mind, and for the most part this has little to do with what we want. Even if they perform a trick on command it's done less to please us and more to obtain the treat they expect afterward. This makes the concept of punishment difficult for them to understand.

Punishment is an area of constant contention and discussion amongst the companion bird community. Some recommend punishments in a variety of forms that the bird finds unpleasant (such as a squirt of water in response to an unwanted behavior) however most experts caution against this, insisting that the bird will not connect the punishment with its behavior but will simply associate the bad experience with YOU PERSONALLY and this will be detrimental to your relationship. This is good advice when the bird is engaging in natural bird behavior like chewing on things or throwing food. The fact that you don't want them to shred your college diploma will never occur to them and if you punish them for doing so they won't be able to understand why. Their focus would be on the action (chewing), not the object on which they're performing that action (your diploma). It would be tantamount to spanking a child for being hungry. It just doesn't make sense. As the half of the human/bird relationship that puts value on your college diploma, and understanding that birds need to chew things up, it's your responsibility to put that diploma where the bird isn't able to reach it.

On the other hand, there are definitely behaviors that need to be dealt with, such as screaming. If "Shriekymouth" has learned that every time he screams you run into the room and shout at him, screaming becomes a satisfactory way to ensure you'll come by. In effect, the bird thinks he has trained *you* to respond to his screaming. It doesn't matter whether or not you shout at him or squirt him with water when you appear. As the old saying goes, "negative attention is still attention." The experts insist that the best way to stop such behavior is to IGNORE it, in the same way one should ignore a child throwing a tantrum. Eventually, when the solicited reaction does not occur, the bird (or child) will stop using up all that energy to shriek and carry on because it isn't getting them what they wanted. (The hard part is living through the ordeal until the undesired behavior EVENTUALLY becomes extinct. It's that "eventually" which is the hardest to endure!)

Many bird behaviorists claim that birds don't understand the concept of punishment at all. In my mind, while they accept "punishments" and other negative events stoically, I think the concept doesn't make sense to them however I believe they understand **consequences** to some extent. Here's what I mean: When I accidentally hurt Dorian while preening his new quills he'll turn around and nip me. Is this punishment meted out by the bird? A warning? Sort of a "you hurt me so the consequence is that now I'm going to hurt you" exchange? Well, maybe and maybe not. Since Dorian considers me his mate he accepts actions from me that he won't accept from Al. For example, being only human, sometimes I lose patience with what I consider Dorie's misbehavior so I'll verbally reprimand him but if he's really pushed too far I'll sometimes take the "bad bath" mister (which is set to thin spray instead of mist) and wet him down, which he happens to dislike. This serves as a complete distraction to him and he'll quickly forget to continue the annoying behavior and will stay quietly in his cage while he dries off and I cool off. Because he thinks of me as his mate he won't hold this apparently aggressive action against me. In fact sometimes I believe he knows he's pushed too far because he'll start calling to me in his "I'm just a sweet little innocent baby bird" voice, giving me lot of "big kiss" sounds and cajolingly saying "Dorie good bird" and other placating phrases (though he's never said "sorry"). There is never any reaction that indicates a new hesitation or fear on his part.

He accepts that I got angry at him (whether he understands why or not) but now the event is over. Since my bathing him this way has never actually stopped him from repeating the same behavior, one can assume that my doing so has only helped ME get over my anger and not taught Dorian anything.

This does NOT mean we condone doing such things with any other creature! Each animal has its own character and any other bird in the world might act differently with another human. I'm simply stating what goes on between Dorian and me. When Al disciplines the bird, Dorian reacts differently – seemingly remaining angry with Al for a longer period of time but again, once they've cooled off, their relationship resumes just as it was before the unhappy encounter.

Isolating Dorian, or giving him a "time out" in his sleeping box is a punishment we use however it doesn't teach him not to repeat the undesired behavior; all it really accomplishes is giving us ten minutes of relative quiet while his dark, quiet surroundings distract him from whatever behavior caused the hubbub in the first place. Like we said in the section called "The Most Difficult Concepts to Teach a Bird", the idea that their actions have consequences is something that either Dorian doesn't really comprehend, or is simply viewed as "the price" of certain behaviors.

As a last word, it's important to consider that "Human Abuse" can be just as damaging as animal abuse, and when living with "Screechy" has become more grief than grand, more pain than pleasure you need to step back and think things through. It is never acceptable to hurt any animal of any species (humans included) so alternative choices must be understood and if appropriate, considered.

Though we humans can be loving caretakers and parents to our pets we should never be so unrealistically giving that we continue to endure more stress than joy. We live with other species because we derive pleasure and fulfillment from doing so. Realistically, all relationships have their ups and downs but if the "downs" start to seriously outweigh the "ups", it may be time to consider severing the relationship.

KNOWING WHEN TO CALL IT QUITS

It's like we said at the very beginning. Parrots and other psitticines are very long-lived birds and deciding to live with them involves a lifelong commitment. They are not a "sometimes" thing to be played with only when you feel like it then ignored the rest of the time. They won't let that happen! They'll loudly TELL you about it when they feel neglected.

They are most certainly NOT accessories to be carried about because they attract attention sitting on your shoulder. It will attract more attention when they poop on your Vera Wang blouse and more yet if they're startled and either shriek loudly enough to deafen you or end up biting into your earlobe – or worse – into your beautiful or handsome face!

Birds are NOT independent and self-contained the way cats can be, and they are NOT accommodating and eager-to-please the way dogs are (We know – we've lived with dogs and cats too). Birds have rules and behaviors they developed over many millions of years and they do not adapt to change any better than we humans do. The world is seen from THEIR point of view only, and they're simply not capable of understanding or considering your needs, desires, and schedule. They are constantly curious and will constantly test their boundaries, and if given the chance they WILL chew on your furniture, throw their food in splatters across your wall, drop half a walnut shell into your shoe, and considerately attempt to pick that mole off your cheek for you.

Birds don't ever grow beyond their natural egocentrism. They will never ask you how YOU feel or how YOUR day went, but they'll want to cuddle with you, be petted by you, sing with you, or just plain stand near you for hours at a time, and if you leave them at the vet while you go on your two week honeymoon, when you get back they'll be quite angry with you for abandoning them.

Birds are messy, demanding, and time-consuming and if you're not willing to commit yourself to the proper care of these fascinating creatures you definitely should NOT obtain one.

But oh, things happen, don't they? Maybe, with all finest intentions in the world you raised a bird and lived happily with it for years. Uh oh, you've found a mate and the bird is so jealous that blood is drawn too often, or your darling is seriously allergic to bird down. What do you do?

Perhaps you've given it your best shot for a year or two and you and the bird just aren't living the happy, affectionate life you imagined. Maybe the neighbors are complaining about the noise the bird makes every morning and evening. Maybe you're too tempted to hit the bird or lock it in a dark closet or not feed it for a few days to see if that "shuts it up".

Maybe you've lived with your bird for many years but you've reached a point where arthritis or other maladies that so often accompany the human aging process make cleaning the cage literally painful. It could happen that over the years, the morning calls have deafened you, the constant cleaning up is hard to do, and your endless well of patience and tolerance is finally running dry.

When do you call it quits and make the call to your local Parrot Rescue facility? It's as difficult a decision as delivering your aged parent to a Nursing Home or surrendering your child to foster parents. Our pets ARE our family but tragically, sometimes it's better for both of you to end the relationship.

We recently read a heart-wrenching story of a Macaw that had lived with one person for all its 40 years but that person had reached their 90s and was succumbing to dementia. When discovered, the bird had been badly physically abused, and not understanding why, it had started to pick its feathers out. Happily, this bird was rescued from this tragic situation and given the reassurance and affection it needed to begin to recover. We never did hear what became of the elderly lady but we certainly hope she also received the care she needed. This was certainly a case where the owner was unable to care for the bird and really needed to give it up for adoption. We prefer to believe her disease prevented her from being able to do so.

Please don't make that sort of mistake. If you really believe you're up to the challenge as well as the rewards of developing a relationship with these magnificent animals try it but do so with both eyes open and give it your best shot for as long as you can. If you find that you just can't do it, or your kids are getting bitten or striking back at the bird, or if you're physically unable to keep up with the necessary cleaning, feeding and attention to keep everyone happy, make the decision. In the long run both you and the bird will end up happier once you both get over the trauma of separation.

How do you give away a bird? There are many, many reputable Parrot Rescue organizations throughout the country who will take custody of the bird, have it examined by an avian vet, and place it in a foster home until it can be adopted by a trained and carefully evaluated new owner. It is far better to surrender a bird to a Rescue organization or Bird Sanctuary than to give it away to a friend who thinks they know what they're getting into, or give it to the SPCA, which will not instruct a potential adopter on what it's like to own a bird and must eventually euthanize it if it's not adopted.

Teaching people what it's really like to live with parrots and other large birds is why we've written this book. EVERY pet of every species deserves the best treatment we can provide, and it is with love and concern that we've tried to prepare anyone considering a parrot or other large bird to understand what is needed to make both you and the bird happy.

🪶A BRIEF WORD ABOUT ROVER AND POLGARA

You might wonder why we've focused so much on Dorian in this book, while often mentioning our two other birds. It's much like having three children, two of which are fine while one becomes a special needs child. Rover and Polgara have already experienced more than one owner.

Al with Rover and Polgara (on his shoulder just for the photo)

As I said at the beginning, we rescued them from someone who was abusing them, and they've bonded with each other for over twenty five years. Though each of them has been scarred by their previous treatment, they depend on one another and can adapt to new situations. They are wonderful birds, though they prefer to spend time with each other rather than with us. In fact, being of two different species from two distinctly different parts of the world, they often don't understand each other, and many an argument or spat has come about because of this. Rover will generously try to give Polgara a toy but he does so by pushing it into her face, which she takes as an assault. Well, I might take it as an assault too. Polgara will want to stop playing with him so she'll try to step away, to which he'll respond by grabbing her by the wing and yanking her back, which once again, she does not take kindly to (and again, neither would I). Despite their daily arguments and shouting matches they love one another and we love them as part of our family. At the same time we have to believe they would be able to more readily adapt to a new family than Dorian would.

Dorian has only known one home and one family and thinks of himself as bonded to Al and me, while Rover and Polgara are "unfavored" flock members. Because of this we feel he will suffer the most upon our inevitable demise, so, as we said at the very beginning, part of the reason we've written this book is to provide a sort of "owner's manual" for the person who takes Dorian into a new home after we're gone.

You might wonder why he wouldn't automatically go to our daughter along with anything else she might inherit from us. She will certainly have that option when the time comes but realistically, it's a matter of logistics. Rachael and her husband both work outside their home; which would leave Dorian home alone with their TWO CATS all day long – a situation fraught with potential peril; especially since the closest the cats have ever been to a bird is to interestedly watch them outside their window. Also, the noise and mess factor of living with birds is something an entire family must be willing to take on. It's asking a lot. I assume our loss would be difficult enough, when the time comes – we don't want to put either Rachael and her family or Dorian into a situation that would make any of them additionally stressed out so we want to make sure other options are available. Our "special needs child" will have to find a home where the trauma of the unavoidable change would be minimized.

AN EVEN BRIEFER WORD ABOUT BIRDS WITH OTHER PETS

A common question about living with companion parrots and their cousins has to do with other species kept as pets. Can "Feathers" get along with "Butch" the dog, "Snowflake" the cat or maybe even "Slither" the snake?

The quickest answer is a flat "NO" but that's not to say it hasn't been done successfully many times. We can't speak from personal experience on this subject but research tends to discourage combining parrots with other species of pets. The simplest reason is that many other pet species are predators, as we've mentioned before, and those instincts can kick in at any moment you're not being vigilant – including at night when you and the bird are sleeping but your mostly-nocturnal cat isn't. Also, don't think any confrontation between pet species will be all one-sided. Parrots are not submissive creatures and if cornered will fight back. No matter which pet comes out on top in a confrontation, both are likely to be seriously injured at the least and blinded, maimed, or killed at the worst.

Another reason to avoid multi-species pets is the attention factor. Birds, as we've pointed out, demand a lot of attention and require a lot of maintenance. If you give adequate time to a bird you may find you're neglecting the dog or cat or whatever, to the detriment of your relationship with that other animal. Divide your time more evenly and jealousies can very easily appear, this time to the detriment of everyone's relationship with everyone else. Don't think for a moment that dogs, cats, and parrots don't develop jealousy – they do so as much as they develop love for us. Even if you don't work and believe you are able to divide your time equally between all your pets, you're going to find it a challenge. Word to the wise.

THE RULES OF LIFE AS SET OUT BY BIRDS

Always keep in mind that birds, which are evolved dinosaurs, made up these rules 350 million years ago. Think they're going to give any credence to HUMAN rules? Not real quickly.

Anything New in the Environment Wants To Eat You

Eating is Social

The Bird on the Highest Perch is the Boss

The Bird Owns Any Place It Can Reach

One Must "Officially" Enter the Flock by Greeting the Other Birds

One Must "Officially" Exit the Flock by Saying Goodbye to the Other Birds

Nap Time is to be Respected

Sunrise is Time to Wake Up

In the Morning Birds Must Announce Their Presence To The World

Sunset is Time to Find a Roost the for Night

In the Evening Birds Should Announce Their Sleeping Spot To The Neighborhood

Being Covered Means Birdies MUST Settle Down for the Night (with exceptions)

"Thank you" is expressed with the Beak

To Greet Another Bird, Touch It's Tongue With Yours**

**** DO NOT ATTEMPT THIS GREETING UNLESS YOU'RE VERY WELL ACQUAINTED WITH THE BIRD, OR YOU ACTUALLY *ARE* ANOTHER BIRD. You COULD get bitten!**

DORIAN'S COMMON-USE VOCABULARY

Though Dorian's vocabulary is actually larger than this, the following is a listing of his most often-used words.

bad	do	mommy	shit
bat	do-do-do-do-do-do (Batman theme)	mommy	stop
bat-bird	doing	more	tail-y
bath	Dorian/Dorie	morning	thank
be	down	my	that
beak/beaky	Dru	night	the
bedtime	duck/ducky	NO!	there
bell	Enough	now	tickle
big	for	oh	time
bird/birdy-bird	girl	okay	to
boingy-boingy-boingy	go	on	up
bonk	good	out	walnut
boo	goodbye/g'bye	over	wanna
bowl	got	owl	want
boy	gummy/gummy bear	peek-a-boo	wash
broom	guy	peeper	way
buck-buck-buck	happy	peeping	what
Bucky	hawk	pet	what's
cage	hello	pirate	where
car	here	Polagro	why
chicken	hey	Polgara	wipe
chocolate	honh-honh-honh (Maurice Chevalier)	potty	Yeah

c'mere	hold	problem	you
come	huh?	puppy dog	your
dammit	I	Quiet!	

SOUNDS & SONGS

"Jingle Bells"	chicken cluck	kiss sound	squeaky furniture
Burp	cough	laser gun	throat clearing
Car alarm	cow moo	laughter	tongue clicking
Cat meow	dog bark	owl hoot	tsk tsk
Car alarm	drip sound	sneeze	various whistles
	Hello Duck Bird		wolf whistle

DORIAN'S MOST COMMON PHRASES

Are you a good duck?

Are you a peeper?

Are you a pirate?

Are you an owl?/ are you a good owl?

Are you my good owl?

Are you ready?/Are you ready there?

Bad Bird!

Be a good boy/be a good bird

Be a hawk

Beak/beaky

beaky wipe/beaky wash

beaky-beaky

Big Cookie

Big Kiss!

Birdy-Bird

Bonk the Bird Beak

Bucky

chicken

chocolate gummy (invented word for fudge)

C'mere

C'mere bird/birdy

Coffee! Coffee! Coffee!

Come on, Duck

Come over here

Damn Bird

Dirty beak

go back up

go in your bowl

Go on

go on up

go potty

Go to the cage

Good ducky/ good duck

Good girl/good boy

Good Morning

Good night/ good night ducky

good, good birdy

Got a kiss for me?

Gummy the chocolate cookie

Happy the Duck Bird

Hello, Hello duck

Hey! Hey you!

Hey, Dru/ hey Rover/ hey Pol

hey, guy/ hey Dorian

hold on

I got the birdy

I got the tail-y

Jingle Bell, jingle all way, oh what a good bird*

jump up

No peeping!

Peek-a-boo! Or peek-a-bird!

Pet the bird

Time to bonk the bird on the beak

up - down (game we play)

up-up-up-up

Wanna come out?

want a bath

Want chocolate

Want Dinner

want go in your bowl

Want gummy

Want gummy bear

Want more

Want that?

want peeping

Want to go to bedtime

What a good bird, what a good boy

What a good duck bird/ducky

What are you doing there?

What are you doing?

what is the birdy doing?

What's your problem?

where are you

where's chocolate gummy

Where's Dorian?

Where's that bird?

Where's the beak?

Where's the bird?

why are you peeping?

Do you want the broom?	Stop peeping	You be a good boo/bird/boy
Dorie the Duck, Dorie Duck/Dorie Duck Bird	thank you	You go for a ride in the car
Dorie, No – No!	Tickle the bird	You want gummy?
Don't you bite me!	tickle tickle	You want peeping?
Duck Bird/Ducky bird	tickle time	You're a good ducky
Go back to the cage		

JUST A FEW OF THE MANY, MANY EXCELLENT ONLINE AND HARD COPY RESOURCES FOR INFORMATION ABOUT COMPANION PARROTS

We strongly encourage you to take advantage of these excellent resources which provide an enormous amount of educational information as well as fascinating articles, breathtaking photos, and fine examples of the heartwarming, funny, and wonderful world of living with companion birds. They are all fantastic resources and just a small sampling of the exemplary informational resources available online and in hard copy.

WEBSITES

http://www.aav.org/ (The Association of Avian Veterinarians)

http://www.avianweb.com/ (Avian Web)

http://www.parrots.org/ (World Parrot Trust)

https://www.facebook.com/pages/Companion-Parrot-Onlinecom/396288143769429 (Companion Parrot Online)

http://www.birdbraingifts.com/ Bird Brain Gifts – Unique Gifts (and wit) by Janet Bray

http://floridaparrotrescue.com/ (Florida Parrot Rescue)

www.birdloversonly.org (Bird Lovers Only Rescue Service)

www.africangreys.com (African Grey Parrot Information)

http://parrotconsultations.blogspot.com (Parrot Behavior & Enrichment consultations)

(http://allcreaturesvetcare.com/index.php (All Creatures Veterinary Care Center, Sewell, NJ)

www.peteducation.com (Pet Education dot com by Drs. Foster and Smith)

www.african-grey-parrot.com (African Grey Parrot dot com)

. http://www.featheredfamily.com/ (Feathered Family, Inc)

http://www.birdsnways.com/wisdom/ww59e.htm (Winged Wisdom Pet Bird Magazine)

BOOKS

The Companion Parrot Handbook, Sally Blanchard, Pet Bird Report, 1999

The Human Nature of Birds, Theodore X Barber, St. Martin's Press, New York, 1994

Good Bird!, Barbara Heidenreich, Avian Publications, 2003

Why Does My Bird Do That? A Guide to Parrot Behavior, Julie Rach Mancini, Wiley Publishing, 2007

ARTICLES

http://news.bbc.co.uk/earth/hi/earth_news/newsid_9382000/9382181.stm "Parrots Prefer Lefthandedness", Emma Brennand, BBC Earth News Feb, 2011 http://news.bbc.co.uk/earth/hi/earth_news/newsid_9382000/9382181.stm "Hand Preference in Humans, Animals Explained" Jennifer Viegas, Discovery News, Feb, 2011

http://news.discovery.com/animals/hand-preference-animals-human-110202.html "Feather Dust and Powder Down Birds" Carol Highfill, Winged Wisdom, Pet Bird Magazine (e-zine), August, 2001

http://www.dailymail.co.uk/sciencetech/article-2185209/How-parrots-smarter-children-monkeys-dogs.html "Who's A Clever Boy, Then? How Parrots Have the Reasoning Skills of a Three Year Old," Fiona Macrae, The Daily Mail Online, , August, 2012..

http://www.care2.com/greenliving/scientists-declare-animals-are-as-aware-as-humans.html Care2 dot com/ "Scientists Declare: Animals Are as Aware as Humans", George Dvorsky, io9.com, via Discovery Channel

http://www.ewg.org/reports/toxicteflon "EWG finds heated Teflon pans can turn toxic faster than DuPont claims", Jane Houlihan, Environmental Working Group, May, 2003

http://yourparrotcage.com/Bird%20Care/Toxic%20to%20your%20Bird.html "Toxic to Birds", Kimberly Santor, The Caged Bird Courier, July 2004 - updated December 2010

http://www.nature.com/news/2009/090731/full/news.2009.760.html "Birds Born to Fear Red" by Matt Kaplan, Nature: The International Weekly Journal of Science, July 31, 2009

Made in the USA
Las Vegas, NV
23 November 2022